CAPRICORN
WITCH

©JAMES C. WELCH

Ivo Dominguez, Jr. (Georgetown, DE) has been active in the magickal community since 1978. He is one of the founders of Keepers of the Holly Chalice, the first Assembly of the Sacred Wheel coven. He currently serves as one of the Elders in the Assembly. Ivo is the author of several books including *The Four Elements of the Wise* and *Practical Astrology for Witches and Pagans*. In his mundane life, he has been a computer programmer, the executive director of an AIDS/HIV service organization, a bookstore owner, and many other things. www.ivodominguezjr.com.

© GAVIN DRUMMOND

Maria Wander (Bronx, NY) is an NYC-based High Priestess, CAP-ISAR-certified consulting astrologer, practicing Astro Mage/herbalist, and a Director for the National Council of Geocosmic Research. Her foci include Hellenistic, Horary, and Uranian astrology. She teaches and is an avid reader of Tarot, Lenormand, and Magi Destiny cards. In her mundane life, she holds a doctorate in Nursing and is a university professor, board-certified nurse informaticist, hypnotherapist, home textiles designer, fiber artist, and mom to two cats and a turtle. www.mariawander.com.

• UNLOCK THE MAGIC OF YOUR SUN SIGN •

CAPRICORN
WITCH

♑

IVO DOMINGUEZ, JR.
MARIA WANDER

Llewellyn Publications
Woodbury, Minnesota

FIRST EDITION
First Printing, 2024

Art direction and cover design by Shira Atakpu
Book design by Christine Ha
Interior art by the Llewellyn Art Department
Tarot Original 1909 Deck © 2021 with art created by Pamela Colman Smith and Arthur Edward Waite. Used with permission of LoScarabeo.
The Capricorn Correspondences appendix is excerpted with permission from *Llewellyn's Complete Book of Correspondences: A Comprehensive & Cross-Referenced Resource for Pagans & Wiccans* © 2013 by Sandra Kynes.

Llewellyn Publications is a registered trademark of Llewellyn Worldwide Ltd.

Library of Congress Cataloging-in-Publication Data (Pending)
ISBN: 978-0-7387-7289-9

Llewellyn Worldwide Ltd. does not participate in, endorse, or have any authority or responsibility concerning private business transactions between our authors and the public.

All mail addressed to the author is forwarded but the publisher cannot, unless specifically instructed by the author, give out an address or phone number.

Any internet references contained in this work are current at publication time, but the publisher cannot guarantee that a specific location will continue to be maintained. Please refer to the publisher's website for links to authors' websites and other sources.

Llewellyn Publications
A Division of Llewellyn Worldwide Ltd.
2143 Wooddale Drive
Woodbury, MN 55125-2989
www.llewellyn.com

Printed in the United States of America

CONTENTS

∙ SPELLS, RECIPES, AND PRACTICES ∙

Ivo Dominguez, Jr.

This is the tenth book in the Witch's Sun Sign series. There are twelve volumes in this series with a book for every Sun sign, but with a special focus on witchcraft. This series explores and honors the gifts, perspectives, and joys of being a witch through the perspective of their Sun sign. Each book has information on how your sign affects your magick and life experiences with insights provided by witches of your Sun sign, as well as spells, rituals, and practices to enrich your witchcraft. This series is geared toward helping witches grow, develop, and integrate the power of their Sun sign into all their practices. Each book in the series has ten writers, so there are many takes on the meaning of being a witch of a particular sign. All the books in the Witch's Sun Sign series are a sampler of possibilities, with pieces that are deep, fun, practical, healing, instructive, revealing, and authentic.

Welcome to the Capricorn Witch

I'm Ivo Dominguez, Jr., and I've been a witch and an astrologer for over forty years. In this book, and in the whole series, I've written the chapters focused on astrological information and collaborated with the other writers. For the sake of transparency, I am a Sagittarius, and most of the other writers for this book are Capricorns.[1] The chapters focused on the lived experience of being a Capricorn witch were written by my coauthor, Maria Wander, who is a High Priestess, an astrologer, an herbalist, a tarot and Lenormand cardslinger, and a nurse. The spells and shorter pieces written for this book come from a diverse group of strong Capricorn witches. Their practices will give you a deeper understanding of yourself as a Capricorn and as a witch. With the information, insights, and methods offered here, your Capricorn nature and your witchcraft will be better united. The work of becoming fully yourself entails finding, refining, and merging all the parts that make your life and identity. This all sounds very serious, but the content of this book will run from lighthearted to profound to do justice to the topic. Moreover, this book has practical suggestions on using the power of your Sun sign to improve your craft as a witch. There are many

1. The exceptions are Dawn Aurora Hunt, who contributes a recipe for each sign in the series, and Sandra Kynes, whose correspondences are listed in the appendix.

books on Capricorn or astrology or witchcraft; this book is about wholeheartedly being a Capricorn witch.

There is a vast amount of material available in books, blogs, memes, and videos targeted at Capricorn. The content presented in these ranges from serious to snarky and a fair amount of it is less than accurate or useful. After reading this book, you will be better equipped to tell which of these you can take to heart and use, and which are fine for a laugh but not much more. There is a good chance that you will be flipping back to reread some chapters to get a better understanding of some of the points being made. This book is meant to be read more than once, and some parts of it may become reference material that you will use for years. Consider keeping a folder, digital or paper, for your notes and ideas on being a Capricorn witch.

What You Will Need

Knowing your Sun sign is enough to get quite a bit out of this book. However, to use all the material in this book, you will need your birth chart to verify your Moon sign and rising sign. In addition to your birth date, you will need the location and the time of your birth as exactly as possible. If you don't know your birth time, try to get a copy of your birth certificate, though not all birth certificates list times. If it is reasonable and you feel comfortable, you can ask family members for information. They may remember an exact time, but even narrowing it down to a range of hours will be useful. There is a solution to not having your exact birth time. Since it takes moments to create birth charts using software, you can run birth charts that are thirty minutes apart over the span of hours that contain your possible birth times. By reading the chapters that describe the characteristics of Moon signs and rising signs, you can reduce the pile of possible charts to a few contenders. Read the descriptions and find the chart whose combination of Moon sign and rising sign rings true to you. There are more refined techniques that a professional astrologer can use to get closer to a chart that is more accurate. However, knowing your Sun sign, Moon sign, and rising sign is all you need for this book. There are numerous websites that offer free basic birth charts you can view online. For a fee, more detailed charts are available on these sites.

You may want to have an astrological wall calendar or an astrological day planner for keeping track of the sign and phase of the Moon. You will want to keep track of what your ruling planet, Saturn, is doing. Over time as your knowledge grows, you'll probably start looking at where all the planets are, what aspects they are making, and when they are retrograde or direct. You could do this all on an app or at a website, but it is often easier to flip through a calendar or planner to see what is going on. Flipping forward and back through the weeks and months ahead can give you a better sense of how to prepare for upcoming celestial influences. Moreover, the calendars and planner contain basic background information about astrology and are a great start for studying astrology.

You're a Capricorn and So Much More

Every person is unique, complex, and a mixture of traits that can clash, complement, compete, or collaborate with each other. This book focuses on your Capricorn Sun sign and provides starting points for understanding your Moon sign and rising sign. It cannot answer all your questions or be a perfect fit because of all the other parts that make you an individual. However, you will find more than enough to enrich and deepen your witchcraft as a Capricorn. There will also be descriptions you won't agree with or that you think do not portray you. In some instances, you will be correct, and in other cases, you may come around to acknowledging that the information does apply to you. Astrology can be used for magick, divination, personal development, and more. No matter what the purpose, your understanding of astrology will change over time as your life unfolds and your experience and self-knowledge broaden. You will probably return to this book several times as you find opportunities to use more of the insights and methods.

This may seem like strange advice to find in a book for the Capricorn witch, but remember that you are more than a Capricorn witch. In the process of claiming the identity of being a witch, it is common to want to have a clear and firm definition of who you are. Sometimes this means overidentifying with a category, such as water witch, herb witch, crystal witch, kitchen witch, and so on. It is useful to become aware of the affinities you have so long as you do not limit and bind yourself to being less than you are. The best use for this book is to uncover all the parts of you that are Capricorn so you can integrate them well. The finest witches I know have well-developed specialties but also are well rounded in their knowledge and practices.

Onward!

With all that said, the Sun is the starting point for your power and your journey as a witch. The first chapter is about the profound influence your Sun sign has, so don't skip through the table of contents; please start at the beginning. After that, Maria will dive into magick and practices that come naturally to Capricorn witches. I'll be walking you through the benefits of picking the right times, places, and things to energize your Capricorn magick. Maria will also share a couple of real-life personal stories of her ups and downs, as well as advice on the best ways to protect yourself spiritually and set good boundaries when you really need to. I'll introduce you to how your Moon sign and your rising sign shape your witchcraft. Maria offers great stories about how her Capricorn nature comes forward in her life as a witch, then gives suggestions on self-care and self-awareness. I'll share a full ritual with you to call on the spirit of your sign. Last, Maria offers her wisdom on how to become a better Capricorn witch. Throughout the whole book, you'll find tables of correspondences, spells, recipes, techniques, and other treasures to add to your practices.

HOW YOUR SUN
POWERS YOUR MAGICK

Ivo Dominguez, Jr.

The first bit of astrology people generally learn is their Sun sign. Some enthusiastically embrace the meaning of their Sun sign and apply it to everything in their life. They feel their Sun is shining and all is well in the world. Then at some point, they'll encounter someone who will, with a bit of disdain, enlighten them on the limits of Sun sign astrology. They feel their Sun isn't enough, and they scramble to catch up. What comes next is usually the discovery that they have a Moon sign, a rising sign, and all the rest of the planets in an assortment of signs. Making sense of all this additional information is daunting as it requires quite a bit of learning and/or an astrologer to guide you through the process. Wherever you are in this or similar journeys into the world of astrology, at some point, you will circle back around and rediscover that the Sun is still in the center.

The Sun in your birth chart shows where life and spirit came into the world to form you. It is the keeper of your spark of spirit and the wellspring of your power. Your Sun is in Capricorn, so that is the flavor, the color, the type of energy that is at your core. You are your whole birth chart, but it is your Capricorn Sun that provides the vital force that moves throughout all parts of your life. When you work in harmony and alignment with your Sun, you have access to more life and the capacity to live it better. This is true for all people, but this advice takes on a special meaning for those who are witches. The root of a witch's magick power is revealed by their Sun sign. You can draw on many kinds of energy, but the type of energy you attract with greatest ease is Capricorn. The more awareness and intention you apply to connecting with and acting as a conduit for that Capricorn Sun, the more effective you will be as a witch.

The more you learn about the meaning of a Capricorn Sun, the easier it will be to find ways to make that connection. To be effective in magick, divination, and other categories of workings, it is vital that you understand yourself, your motivations, drives, attractions, and so on so that you can refine your intentions, questions, and desired outcomes. Understanding your Sun sign is an important step in that process. One of the goals shared by both witchcraft and astrology is to affirm and to integrate the totality of your nature to live your best life. The glyph for the Sun in astrology is a dot with a circle around it. Your Capricorn Sun is the dot and the circle, your center, and your circumference. It is your beginning and your journey. It is also the core of your personal Wheel of the Year, the seasons of your life that repeat, have resonances, but are never the same.

How Capricorn Are You?

The Sun is the hub around which the planets circle. Its gravity pulls the planets to keep them in their courses and bends space-time to create the place we call our solar system. The Sun in your birth chart tugs on every other part of your chart in a similar way. Everything is both bound and free, affected but seeking its own direction. When people encounter descriptions of Capricorn traits, they will often begin to make a list of which things apply to them and which don't. Some will say that they are the epitome of Capricorn traits, others will claim that they are barely Capricorn, and many will be somewhere in between. Evaluating how closely or not you align with the traditional characteristics of a Capricorn is not a particularly useful approach to understanding your sign. If you are a Capricorn, you have all the Capricorn traits somewhere within you. What varies from person to person is the expression of those traits. Some traits express fully in a classic form, others are blocked from expressing or are modified, and sometimes there is a reaction to behave as the opposite of what is expected. As a Capricorn and especially as a witch, you have the capacity to activate dormant traits, shape functioning traits, and tone down overactive traits.

The characteristics and traits of signs are tendencies, drives, and affinities. Gravity encourages a ball to roll down a hill. A plant's leaves will grow in the direction of sunlight. The warmth of a fire will draw people together on a cold night. A flavor you enjoy will entice you to take another bite of your food. Your Capricorn Sun urges you to be and to act like a Capricorn. That said, you also have free will and volition to make other choices. Moreover, the rest of your birth chart and the ever-changing celestial influences are also shaping your options, moods, and drives. The more you become aware of the traits and behaviors that come with being a Capricorn, the easier it will be to choose how you express them. Most people want to be able to choose how they express themselves and how they make their mark on the world, but for a Capricorn, this is essential for their well-being.

As a witch, you have additional tools to work with the Capricorn energy. You can choose when to access and how you shape the qualities of Capricorn as they come forth in your life. You can summon the energy of Capricorn, name the traits you desire, and manifest them. You can also banish or neutralize or ground what you don't need. You can find where your Capricorn energy short-circuits, where it glitches, and unblock it. You can examine your uncomfortable feelings and your less-than-perfect behaviors to seek the shadowed places within so you can heal or integrate them. Capricorn is a spirit and a current of collective consciousness that is vast in size. Capricorn is also a group mind and archetype. Capricorn is not limited to humanity; it engages with plants, animals, minerals, and all the physical and nonphysical beings of the Earth and all its associated realms. As a witch, you can call upon and work with the spiritual entity that is Capricorn. You can live your life as a ritual. The motion of your life can be a dance to the tune and rhythm of the heavens.

The Capricorn Glyph

The glyph for Capricorn has many variants and they are all a bit more complicated than the other astrological glyphs. The two variants shown have proven to be the most effective for magickal purposes. The Capricorn glyph can be seen as spirit descending swiftly into matter, into incarnation. The trajectory is so steep it misses the mark and falls all the way into the depths of the sea. The sea goat of Capricorn must now climb from the depths of the sea to the heights of the mountain. Once the summit of the mountain is reached, there is an epiphany. Then another descent, but one informed by grace and understanding to begin the cycle again. In the pictographic code of the astrological glyphs, curves represent the journey of the work of integration, circles and loops represent spirit, and semi-circles represent soul. Spirit is the part of you that is eternal, and soul is the part that is shaped and changed by the experiences of incarnation. All the variants are a complex mixture of these punctuated with sharp turns and a crossroads. Since Capricorn's work is really the Great Work of spiritual alchemy, the glyph can be seen as a road map.

With the use of your imagination, you can see this glyph as representing the sea goat. Some people say the circle or loop is the kneecap since Capricorn rules the knees. The shape of the glyph can also remind you that the journey through life has many twists, turns, and setbacks. This is often one of the hardest glyphs for students to learn to draw consistently until they have drawn it many times. This difficulty is very much a Capricorn lesson in determination to become proficient.

By meditating on the glyph, you will develop a deeper understanding of what it is to be a Capricorn. You may also come up with your own personal gnosis or story about the glyph that can be a key that is uniquely yours. The glyph for Capricorn can be used as a sigil to call or concentrate its power. The glyph for Capricorn can be used in a similar fashion to the scribing of an invoking pentacle that is used to open the gates to the elemental realms. However, instead of the elemental realms, this glyph opens the way to the realms of mind and spirit that are the source of Capricorn. To make this glyph work, you need to deeply ingrain the feeling of scribing this glyph. Visually it is complicated, so memorizing it will take a bit longer, but having a kinesthetic feel for it turns it into magick. Spend some time doodling the glyph on paper. Try drawing the glyph on your palm with a finger for several repetitions as that adds several layers of sensation and memory patterns.

Whenever you need access to more of your magickal energy, scribe the Capricorn glyph in your mind, on your hand, in the air, however you can. Then pull, channel, and feel your center fill with whatever you need. It takes very little time to open this connection using the glyph. Consider making this one of the practices you use to get ready to do divination, spell work, ritual, or just to start your day.

Capricorn Patterns

This is a short list of patterns, guidelines, and predilections for Capricorn Sun people to get you started. If you keep a book of shadows, or a journal, or files on a digital device to record your thoughts and insights on magickal work, you may wish to create your own list to expand upon these. The process of observing, summarizing, and writing down your own ideas in a list is a great way to learn about your sign.

- You are known for ambition, the capacity to work hard, and keeping your composure in the midst of tempests. What is less known is that when you let your hair down, you party harder than all the rest or take off on a vacation like a rocket.

- The universe rarely cuts a Capricorn any slack. This is one of the reasons that Capricorns are said to be practical planners, because if they don't abide by the limits of the world, they are quickly reminded.

You can be stoic, work hard, and persevere to reach your goals, but you would be wise to rest and recover as needed. Let's compare your efforts to physical fitness programs. It is in the rest day between the exercise when you build strength, and too much effort results in losses, not gains.

When you are on the clock, on task, you can be cold, clinical, and stony. When it comes to close friends and family, you are caring and dutiful, but make sure you add them to the schedule.

Lists of traits for the signs will often unfairly typify Capricorns as being overly materialistic. This is a very spiritual earth sign who knows they incarnated to learn the lessons of being on the planet. Embracing the material is a central part of the spiritual work.

Capricorns feel the pressure of time more keenly than others. In part, this is because it is easy to feel behind schedule because you've taken on so much. The good news is that Capricorns tend to age well and become younger in spirit as time goes on.

Traditions matter to you, give you comfort, and you do your best to keep them alive. You may be conservative or progressive; Capricorns come in every political or philosophical flavor. However, you will do your best to keep a line of continuity and conversation between the past, the present, and the future.

You like to be in control of as many variables in your life as you can. If you don't or can't exert the level of control you need, you may get anxious or depressed. Learning to share power with others and to collaborate will resolve many dilemmas.

Learning new skills, trying a new physical activity, creating art, hiking, or anything else recreational that also yields accomplishments and new connections is good for you. Moreover, you can convince yourself to take time to do them because they bring added value to your life.

Perfectionism is a problem. Remember that nothing can be truly perfect in the physical plane. Then praise yourself for how close you got to perfection and how clever you were along the way to your successes.

At times you may be concerned that you are too judgmental. Capricorns constantly observe, measure, and judge everything around them. This comes from a need to know the resources, challenges, and options available to make good choices. Judgment and discernment are value neutral until you apply them. Act with integrity and kindness and you'll be fine.

Your peak moments, epiphanies, and flashes of insight are gifts to be treasured and heeded.

Capricorn Sun gives you the ability to do what is needed no matter how difficult the situation. When you take the easy way out, the Sun's powers usually desert you.

You know you can't complete the many tasks you have chosen without including other people. However, to remain healthy, you need to have regular periods of quiet and solitude.

You have a love-hate relationship with structures, hierarchies, organizations. You like to know the ground rules so that you can use them, bend them, or break them.

You are drawn like a moth to a flame to trials that give you an opportunity to test your mettle and prove your worth.

Character and integrity matter a great deal to you. The hardest challenges to keeping true to and improving yourself will not be your work, it will be learning to release emotions and habits that have hardened into barriers on your path.

Despite the strong image you cultivate and the impression you often make on others, you are tenderhearted.

You probably grew up and took on adult responsibilities faster than was ideal. Make time for the child within to flourish as you grow older.

It is admirable that you persevere, work hard, and have high standards. Once you commit to something, you stay the course. As such, it is critical that you take your time to choose wisely. Otherwise, you may squander precious time and energy.

Cardinal Earth

The four elements come in sets of three. The modalities known as cardinal, fixed, and mutable are three different flavors or styles of manifestation for the elements. The twelve-fold pattern that is the backbone of astrology comes from the twelve combinations produced from four elements times three modal-ities. As you go around the wheel of the zodiac, the order of the elements is always fire, earth, air, then water; the modalities are always in the order of cardinal, fixed, then mutable. Each season begins in the cardinal modality, reaches its peak in the fixed modality, and transforms to the next season in the mutable modality. The cardinal modality is the energy of creation bursting forth, coming into being, and spreading throughout the world. The fixed modality is the harmonization of energy so that it becomes and remains fully itself and is preserved. The mutable modality is the energy of flux that is flexibility, transformation, death, and rebirth.

Capricorn is the tenth sign in the zodiac, so it is earth of the cardinal modality. This is why a Capricorn witch can call up the power to rally their resources and get to work so quickly. As a Capricorn witch, you can call upon earth in all its forms; it is easiest to draw upon cardinal earth.

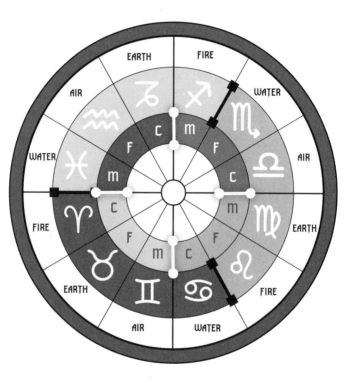

The elements and modalities on the wheel

Saturn, Your Ruling Planet

Your Sun sign determines the source and the type of energy that you have in your core. The ruling planet for a sign reveals your go-to moves and your intuitive or habitual responses for expressing that energy. Your ruling planet provides a curated set of prebuilt responses and custom-tailored stances for you to use in day-to-day life. The name of this planet may suggest the Greek Cronus, the Roman Saturn, or perhaps Father Time, or the rites of Saturnalia. Although this offers some insight, Saturn's role is more like that of a demanding coach or mentor who pushes you to do better. Saturn is your sense of right and wrong and the inner structures that shape your perceptions and actions. Saturn rules time, all patterns, forms, and the limits and powers of the physical plane. Saturn is tasked with enforcing the principle of cause and effect. Since Capricorn is a cardinal earth sign, Saturn urges you to be a mover, a shaker, and an architect of your destiny. All deities related to organizing the world, making judgments, time, aging, labor, and so on connect to Capricorn through this earthy Saturn. Saturn's glyph suggests a scythe as the bringer of the harvest and death. The glyph is also the cross of matter over the curves of the soul or spirit because, while incarnate, the rules of the physical world prevail. Capricorn likes to wield that scythe for the abundance of the harvest and with the realization that seed must be saved to plant again.

Capricorn witches are more strongly affected by whatever Saturn is doing in the heavens. It is useful to keep track of the aspects that Saturn is making with other planets. You can get basic information on what aspects mean and when they are happening in astrological calendars and online resources. You will feel Saturn retrogrades more strongly than most people, but you can find ways to make them useful periods to determine what is working, needs adjustment, or calls for a reboot. Capricorn witches will notice that the impact of the Saturn retrograde will start and end a few days earlier and later than the listed duration. When Saturn in the heavens is in Capricorn or any earth sign, you will feel more empowered. When Mars is in Capricorn where it is exalted, you feel more drive and motivation. This first step to using the power of Saturn is to pay attention to what it is doing, how you feel, and what is happening in your life. Witches can shift their relationship with the powers that influence them. Your awareness of these powers makes it possible to harness those energies to purposes that you choose. Close your eyes, feel for that power, and channel it into your magick.

Saturn can be as great a source of energy for a Capricorn witch as the element of earth. Although there is some overlap between the qualities and capacities assigned to Saturn and Earth, the differences are greater. Saturn is more focused on patterns, time frames, and the process of interaction between physical things. Earth is the medium that manifests the world that we perceive; it is the memory of cumulative changes and seeks stability. Saturn has the power to suggest adaptations and accommodations that allow you to work in the world of matter with finesse. Earth is the ground of being that provides the experiences that are life. Saturn is all patterns, not just physical ones, so information, archetypes, the laws of nature, and so on are in its care. Saturn is all the obstacles and challenges that offer the possibility of triumph in the end. Earth is the principle of manifestation, contraction, and crystallization. Earth provides the limits that provoke wisdom, and Saturn is wisdom. Over time you can map out the overlapping regions and the differences between Saturn and Earth. Using both planetary and elemental resources can give you a much broader range and more finesse.

Capricorn and the Zodiacal Wheel

The order of the signs in the zodiac can also be seen as a creation story where the run of the elements repeats three times. Capricorn is in the last third of the zodiac, the third run of the four elements in the story of the universe. At this stage in their existence, the goal of the elements is to become fully connected to each other and to higher guidance to become organized. Capricorn remembers their purposes for coming into being. The earth of Capricorn builds, establishes instructions, and crystallizes gains. It evaluates the unfolding of the possibilities of existence to find the best route forward. Although Capricorn is sometimes stereotyped as being too negative or rigid, the deeper truth is that they truly understand what is at stake in life and the value of stoicism. Although true for all witches,

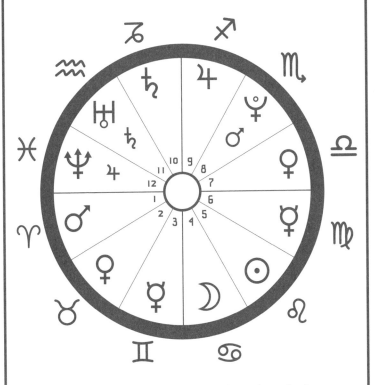

The sign and planet rulers on the zodiac wheel

the Capricorn witch needs to let go of harsh self-judgment, cultivate patience, and trust the power that dwells within them. When you can consistently connect with your Capricorn nature that is your most authentic self, you have all the power you need. You can make progress in this quest through meditation and inner journeys, but that alone will not do. The Capricorn witch learns by doing, by practice, and by being productive in the world. When a Capricorn witch connects to the spiritual qualities of earth, they become the sovereign that governs the constant state of change that is life and encourages evolution.

CAPRICORN
CORRESPONDENCES

♑

Power: To Utilize

Keyword: Maturity

Roles: Architect, Strategist, Manager

Ruling Planet: Saturn ♄

Element: Cardinal Earth

Colors: Black, Grayish Metallics, Dark Neutrals, and Earth Tones

Shape: Triangle

Metals: Lead

Body Part Ruled: Knees and Bones

Day of the Week: Saturday

Affirmation:

I will achieve my goals, but not at the cost of health or love.

WITCHCRAFT THAT COMES NATURALLY TO A CAPRICORN

Maria Wander

Harnessing the natural magicks are fundamental for the Capricorn witch. As one of the earth signs, we are organically part of nature, intrinsically linked to the land, the plants, the rocks, and the temporal order of time and place. We are grounded, practical, steady, capable, salt of the earth, at our best when connecting structurally with the physical plane.

When I was a kid, I'd collect flowers and stones that called to me while I ambled unshod. I'd press the blooms in diaries and line up rocks on my windowsill. I still do this and find my selections are meaningful, instinctively choosing items that support a timely need for grounding, boosting creativity, or adopting change. The Capricornian capacity to manage earthy connections with the forces gathered in plants, crystalline minerals, and loamy spaces is innate to us.

Rulership by Saturn provides Capricorns with the ability to regulate boundaries, which include frontiers of land, sea, and space. The mythic image of the sea goat comprised of a horn-headed ibex with the tail of a fish is a notable, ancient depiction of Capricorn's constellation. This creature portrays our accord with the eternal cosmic firmament and meteoric atoms that originate oceans and mountains. The witchcraft intrinsic to our very natures is that which deeply connects humans with the sum and substance of the natural world. The following practices go hand in hand, and you'll find that you have a gift when it comes to their application.

Green Magick

Plants can form incenses, anointing oils, altar pieces, potions, washes, tinctures, and tools to energize rituals and spells with the green magick of nature. Earth signs are facile channels for green magick and plant communication. Press an herb to keep in your daily journal or create a flower essence. To discern the magickal characteristics of a plant, herb, or flower, you need only ask by communing with its deva, the nurturing spirit of green intelligence.

Start with a Capricorn herb like rosemary or tarragon. Bring attention to your auric field by rubbing your palms together to warmly activate their sensitivity. Hold your palms shoulder width apart, facing toward each other, and slowly bring them together until you can feel auric energy between

them. Face your palms toward the plant, request connection, ask your question, and patiently listen.

Plants are coded with properties that support the harmonious organization of energetic
structures seen in sequential cycles throughout
nature and the cosmos. Saturn as god of
agriculture rules the sequential cycles of seed
and harvest; his glyph is a scythe, the agricultural tool for harvest. "As you sow, so shall
you reap" imparts the downfalls and benefits
of return on investment. Smart farmers under-
take planting when the sign of Capricorn is in
influence for a successful, abundant yield. Radish
can be empowered and eaten for personal accountability
by setting intentions to avoid procrastination and keep
timely motivation to a task. Use corn or cucumber as yin magnetic attractors and spinach or oat as yang active stimulants.
Use carrot for clarity to see true or radish to distinguish a fleet-
ing passion from a steady relationship.

Crystal Magick

Crystal magick employs gems and stones whose structural
organization imparts frequency, vibration, and energy through
color and construct. These rocks are the bones of the Earth and
Saturnian in nature, appearing to be at a standstill but some
actually oscillating with pulsations so regular you can literally

set your watch by them. Quartz is one such, seemingly lifeless but animate in its own right. The first quartz wristwatch was unveiled on December 25, 1969, a tool of time appropriately ushered in on a Capricorn date. The ability of quartz to function in this timepiece is due to piezoelectric polarization of electrons that results from the application of mechanical stress. This is Saturnian in its boundaries of compression, time, and tension.

Just as coals become diamonds under duration and duress, Capricorn natives are attuned to working with crystals as both express resiliency under pressure, dynamically managing stress and mastering time toward worthy outcomes. Carry or make gem essences from crystals whose lore and uses are related to Capricorn or Saturn matters of endurance, perseverance, ambition, and concentration; goldstone, carnelian, and malachite are recommended.

Time Magick

The proverb "the best time to plant a tree was twenty years ago; the second-best time is now" was probably authored by a time-conscious Capricorn. Capricorn crests the top of the astrology chart and caps the end and beginning of the calendar year. Cap ushers in the next Father Time as Baby New Year, whose pure potential is ready to be realized with resolve and a plan in place. Capricorns know that time is not just measurement on a watch, but also a flavor or tone of a moment, like the right time or the best time. Cronus time is calendar time, the time of personal planning, free will selection, and choice. Kairos time is symbolic time, the time of karma and cosmos, the time of quickening when one's first undulations in the maternal waters of birth were felt by mother. Time magick uses calendar time and symbolic time to action on our interests.

Just as the celestial lights of the brilliant Sun and reflective Moon create a rhythm of activity during the daytime and restful sleep at nighttime, there is an ancient system of time called planetary hours that aligns the seven classical planets with the activities they symbolize. Planetary hours are based on the ancient Chaldean order of planets that rule each day of the week and divide day and night into time segments of equal length. This order begins at the end with Saturn, the farthest planet that can still be seen with the naked eye, followed by Jupiter, Mars, Sun, Venus, Mercury, Moon, and returning again to Saturn for another cycle. Planetary hours are calculated by dividing the light half of the day from sunrise to sunset by twelve and the dark half of the day from sunset to sunrise by twelve. The first hour on Monday begins at sunrise with a Moon period to match the planetary day. The remaining planetary hours cycle through in Chaldean order until the next day of the week's sunrise to begin again with the ruling planet for that day, Mars for Tuesday, Mercury for Wednesday, Jupiter for Thursday, Venus for Friday, Saturn for Saturday, and Sun for Sunday.

On Saturday, Saturn would be the first hour, followed by
Jupiter, Mars, Sun, Venus, Mercury, Moon, and beginning at
Saturn hour again and repeating for the remaining seventeen
hours of the day. The order of the planets never changes. For
love magick, choose Venus day, Friday, and/or Venus hour. If
your heart yearns for a lover with Venus in solar Leo, choose
Sunday at Venus hour to place a love call on the astral. For
Venus in Gemini, work magick on Wednesday, Mercury's
day, and do it twice since Mercury loves do-overs. Conduct
Venus hour rites, one at the daytime Venus hour and again
at the nighttime Venus hour. Use Mars for motivation and
amping energy; Jupiter for luck and wisdom; Saturn for mastery, discipline, and responsibility; the Moon for matters of
home and hearth, emotional or psychic concerns; and the
Sun for visibility, success, and empowerment.

Deities and Spirits

Burn Saturnian incense of frankincense, myrrh, cedar, sandalwood, or patchouli to propitiate these deities and spirits
that embody aspects of Capricorn.

For Green Magick

 Chiron—Noble centaur of wisdom, astrology,
prophecy, herbs, and medicine. Unlike other war-
ring centaurs, his front legs were those of a man.
Son of Cronus and sea nymph Philyra, he was a
famed teacher who sacrificed immortality to free

Prometheus and was placed in the heavens as a constellation.

Rhea—Greek goddess of tranquility, productivity, fruitfulness. She planted the Grove of Dodona that spoke prophecies. Wife to Cronus, she bore the Olympians.

For Crystal Magick

Saturn—Astrological energies of boundaries, compression, time, tension, endurance, perseverance, concentration, and ambition. Roman god of agriculture, fertility, harvest, and the cycles of time. Son of Caelus the sky and Tellus the Earth, his mythology mirrors that of Cronus. His festival, Saturnalia, celebrates winter solstice.

For Time Magick

Pricus—The original sea goat, immortal ruler of time, and son of Cronus. Part goat and part amphibian, Pricus was a skilled thinker and speaker whose children's fish tails became goat legs when on land as they lost their skillful mentation and speech. Pricus would turn back time to continue their connection with the sea but ultimately they chose land, losing their dual nature. Cronus placed Pricus into the sea of stars to keep his pelagic origins and abilities.

For Removing Obstacles, Endings, and New Beginnings

Cronus—Greek personification of time itself. Represented as an old man holding a sickle, he leads Titans born of Gaea/Earth and Ouranos/heavens. Ouranos fathered many Titans with Gaea, but his cruelty led her to fashion a sickle for Cronus who castrated Ouranos, separating heaven from Earth, beginning a golden age for mortals.

Janus—Roman god of gates, borders, margins, entrances and exits, initiations and conclusions. His festival was held in January. Activations were sacred to him, his name invoked at start of day, month, year, and any venture. His two-faced visage was placed on gates to bless the commencement and return of a journey. Honor him at New Year's when we review the past and envision the future.

Divination

Divination is an efficient, matter-of-fact process for earthy Capricorns. A great favorite is the thirty-six-card *Petite Lenormand* deck of cards, named after the Napoleonic-era cartomancer, Marie Anne Lenormand. The clarity in the tough love, predictive, concrete communication that comes through in Lenormand cards makes them a Cappy darling. Lenormand cards are read by combining card meanings in a sequential order of A-subject, B-verb, and C-object or modifier with connectors such as *and*, *but*, *with*, *for*, *about*, *to*, and so on or using the card image to show how it affects surrounding cards. The Scythe card point shows where danger or a cut may be. The Book card spine faces secrets and its pages point toward information that may come to light.

Say you're heading to the US nation's capital for a vacation with your beau. He is out sightseeing. Before you call to locate him, you do a three-card spread, pulling cards (A) House, (B) Book, and (C) Key. Read A + B, B + C, A + C, and A + B + C. Key unlocks the important or shows that there is a solution. So, you may actually find him! House + Book = sightsee at a bookstore? House + Key = major establishment—the White House? Book + Key = solving the unknown, important books.

House + Book = library! House + Book + Key. House of important books = ah, the Library of Congress!

How the experience of life can be read through a combination of these cards is astounding. Practice with a three-card spread, then move on to spreads of five and seven cards. All thirty-six cards in a huge spread is aptly called the Grand Tableau, which uses card placements to attach an additional layer to these meanings:

1. Rider: News, local transport, a quick communication, or a young man.
2. Clover: A lucky moment, start of a short-term benefit or spontaneous business venture.
3. Ship: Long-distance travel or a commercial endeavor.
4. House: Dwelling, building, place of comfort, family.
5. Tree: Health, illness, growth.
6. Clouds: Confusion, ambiguity, setbacks, bad weather, smoke.
7. Snake: Confusing path, pipes, devious rivalry.
8. Coffin: Illness, negativity, endings, a box.
9. Bouquet: Gift, surprise, joyful event, invitation.
10. Scythe: Pain, danger, sharp, aggression, harvest.
11. Whip: Controversy, argument, repetition, exercise, having sex.

12. Birds: Verbalized communications, telephone call, pairs, anxiety.
13. Child: New start, innocence, small beginning.
14. Fox: Fraud, harassment, devious cleverness, underhand.
15. Bear: Authority, power, success that breeds jealousy, abundance.
16. Stars: Guidance, clarity, goals, intuition, spirituality.
17. Stork: Change, transformation, relocation, moving, childbirth.
18. Dog: Comrade, trusted companion, loyal friend.
19. Tower: Stability, organization, big building, ambition, legal issues, discipline.
20. Garden: The public, a gathering, society.
21. Mountain: Obstacle, barrier, separation, wall, uphill, weight.
22. Crossroads: Difficult decision, options.
23. Mice: Theft, loss, desecration, filth.
24. Heart: Love, affection, strong feelings.
25. Ring: Accord, marriage, partnership, circle, jewelry, routine.
26. Book: Learning, information, education, secrets, books.
27. Letter: Written message, documents, email, text, data.

28. Man: Anima, masculine characteristics.
29. Woman: Animus energy, feminine characteristics.
30. Lily: Harmony, patron, mentorship, support, making love.
31. Sun: Energy, success, brightness, summer, great luck, daytime.
32. Moon: Illumination, acknowledgment, honors, nighttime.
33. Key: Solution, important, creates an opening or entry.
34. Fish: Money, finances, water, fish, drink, business, management.
35. Anchor: Stability, security and success ensured, maritime, destination reached.
36. Cross: Fate, grief, burden, pain, religion.

The Box Spread

Ask your question. Pull nine cards, placing them left to right in three rows:

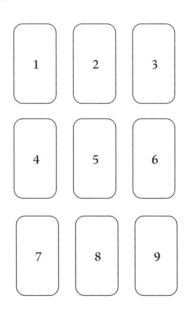

Rows:

- ✦ Cards 1, 2 & 3—conscious thoughts, ideas, ambitions
- ✦ Cards 4, 5 & 6—reality as it exists, daily life
- ✦ Cards 7, 8 & 9—subconscious thoughts and emotions

- ✦ Card 5—center card is the situation or theme of the reading
- ✦ Cards 1, 3, 7 & 9—frame context of the situation, act as influences; read clockwise or in pairs
- ✦ Card 1 sets the fuse; 5 is the focal point that is influenced by every other card; 9 is where the story goes.

Columns:

- ✦ Cards 1, 4 & 7—the past
- ✦ Cards 2, 5 & 8—the present
- ✦ Cards 3, 6 & 9—the future

MAGICAL
CORRESPONDENCES
Maria Wander

♑

As a Capricorn, there are particular types of magikcal processes that are in alignment with our elemental earth vibe and initiating cardinal modality. The kinds of magick we appreciate are in active pursuit of magickal realization, of daily needs and long-term goals. We are practical, tactile, solution-seeking, and focused on initiating and managing the material. Consequently, our spells have a strong, solid basis in the natural, physical world spaces and places.

Types of Spellcraft

- Amulets, charms, and talismans
- Coin magick
- Crystal magick
- Textile magick and poppets
- Augury and scapulimancy
- Earth elemental workings
- Herbalism and communing with devas of flowers, plants, trees, stones

Magical Tools

+ Altars
+ Staffs and wands
+ Besoms
+ Herb crowns
+ Crystal grids
+ Pentacle patens

Magical Goals and Spell Ideas

+ Financial magick
+ Protection spells
+ Magick for time management or organization
+ Productivity and efficiency spells
+ Spells for honoring boundaries
+ Intentional cartomancy
+ Astrological phylactery

Ivo Dominguez, Jr.

Y ou've probably encountered plenty of charts and lists in books and online cataloging which things relate to your Sun sign and ruling planet. There are many gorgeously curated assortments of herbs, crystals, music playlists, fashions, sports, fictional characters, tarot cards, and more that are assigned to your Sun sign. These compilations of associations are more than a curiosity or for entertainment. Correspondences are like treasure maps to show you where to find the type and flavor of power you are seeking. Correspondences are flowcharts and diagrams that show the inner occult relationships between subtle energies and the physical world. Although there are many purposes for lists of correspondences, there are two that are especially valuable to becoming a better Capricorn witch. The first is to contemplate the meaning of the correspondences, the ways in which they reveal meaningful details about your Sun sign and ruling planet, and how they connect to you. This will deepen your understanding of what it is to be a Capricorn witch. The second is to use these items as points of connection to access energies and essences that support your witchcraft. This will expand the number of tools and resources at your disposal for all your efforts.

Each of the sections in this chapter will introduce you to a type of correlation with suggestions on how to identify and use them. These are just starting points, and you will find many more as you explore and learn more. As you broaden your knowledge, you may find yourself a little bit confused as you find that sources disagree on the correlations. These contradictions are generally not a matter of who is in error but a matter of perspective, cultural differences, and the intended uses for the correlations. Anything that exists in the physical world can be described as a mixture of all the elements, planets, and signs. You may be a Capricorn, but depending on the rest of your chart, there may be strong concentrations of other signs and elements. For example, if you find that a particular herb is listed as associated with both Capricorn and Taurus, it is because it contains both natures in abundance. In the cases of strong multiple correlations, it is important that you summon or tune in to the one you need.

Times

You always have access to your power as a Capricorn witch, but there are times when the flow is stronger, readily available, or more easily summoned. There are sophisticated astrological methods to select dates and times that are specific to your birth chart. Unless you want to learn quite a bit more astrology or hire someone to determine these for you, you can do quite well with simpler methods. Let's look at the cycles of the solar year, the lunar month, and the hours of day-night rotation. When the Sun is in Capricorn, or the Moon is in Capricorn, or it is past midnight, you are in the sweet spot for tuning in to the core of your power.

Capricorn season is roughly December 21 to January 20, but check your astrological calendar or ephemeris to determine when it is for a specific year in your time zone. The amount of energy that is accessible is highest when the Sun is at the same degree of Capricorn as it is in your birth chart. This peak will not always be on your birth date, but very close to it. Take advantage of Capricorn season for working magic and for recharging and storing up energy for the whole year.

The Moon moves through the twelve signs every lunar cycle and spends around two and half days in each sign. When the Moon is in Capricorn, you have access to more lunar power because the Moon in the heavens has a resonant link to the Sun in your birth chart. At some point during its time in Capricorn, the Moon will be at the same degree as your Sun. For you, that will be the peak of the energy during the Moon's passage through Capricorn that month. While the Moon is in Capricorn, your psychism is stronger, as is your ability to manifest things. When the Moon is at or just past the dark Moon, in any sign, you can draw upon its power more readily because it is resonant to your sign.

The winter solstice in the northern hemisphere is the beginning of Capricorn season. All the cardinal signs mark the beginnings of the seasons, either solstices or equinoxes. The stations of the year, the holidays, are liminal times of transition. The cardinal earth of Capricorn is filled with the drive to evolve and push the limits of the physical world; it is liminal in a different way. Capricorn is the tenth sign of the zodiac, and the zodiac is like a clock. Just past midnight corresponds to the power of Capricorn. If you are detail focused, you might be wondering when "just past midnight" is. This varies with the time of year and with your location, but if you must have a time, think of it as 12:00 a.m. to 2:00 a.m. Or you can use your intuition and feel your way to when the midpoint of the night has passed, when you know that, despite the darkness, the Sun will return. The powers that flow during this time are mysterious, heroic, and filled with possibilities for greater things to come. Plan on using the Capricorn energy of the night's turning tide for inspiration and to feed spells for resourcefulness, lifting melancholy, prosperity, and power.

The effect of these special times can be joined in any combination. For example, you can choose to do work past midnight when the Moon is in Capricorn, or the Sun is in Capricorn past midnight, or the Moon is in Capricorn during Capricorn season. You can combine all three as well. Each of these time groupings will have a distinctive feeling. Experiment and use your instincts to discover how to use these in your work.

Places

There are activities, professions, phenomena, and behaviors that have an affinity, a resonant connection, to Capricorn and its ruling planet, Saturn. These activities occur in the locations that suit or facilitate their expressions. There is magick to be claimed from those places that is earmarked for Capricorn or your ruling planet, Saturn. Just like your birth chart, the world around you contains the influences of all the planets and signs, but in different proportions and arrangements. You can always draw upon Capricorn or Saturn energy, though there are times when it is more abundant depending upon astrological considerations. Places and spaces have energies that accumulate and can be tapped like a battery. Places contain the physical, emotional, and spiritual environments that are created by the actions of the material objects, plants, animals, and people occupying those spaces. Some of the interactions between these things can generate or concentrate the energies and patterns that can be used by Capricorn witches.

If you look at traditional astrology books, you'll find listings of places assigned to Capricorn and Saturn that include locations such as these:

- The offices where matters of finance, health, and laws are determined

- Ruins, abandoned places, ancient sites, and wastelands

- Seats of power, whether they be political, monetary, or religious

- Deeply shadowed places like dense forests, deep ravines, and caverns

These are very clearly linked to the themes associated with Capricorn and Saturn. With a bit of brainstorming and free-associating, you'll find many other less-obvious locations and situations where you can draw upon this power. For example, wherever competitive games of strategy, working on puzzles, and similar pastimes are being enjoyed, or gardening or planning a landscape is occurring, or people are playing musical instruments, a current will be produced that you can plug into. Any situation where you use your intellect and assessments to sort through and organize ideas, objects, or people, or engage in similar intensely focused activities, can become a source of power. All implements or actions related to DIY projects and higher-end crafts like weaving, jewelry making, and woodworking or specialty tools associated with these could also be sources for energy.

While you can certainly go to places that are identified as locations where Capricorn and/or Saturn energy is plentiful to do workings, you can find those energies in many other circumstances. Don't be limited by the idea that the places must be the ones that have a formalized link to Capricorn. Be on the lookout for Capricorn or Saturn themes and activities wherever you may be. Remember that people thinking, feeling, and participating in activities connected to your sign and its ruling planet are raising power. If you can identify with it as resonating with your Sun sign or ruling planet, then you can call the power and put it to use. You complete the circuit to engage the flow with your visualization, intentions, and actions.

Plants

Capricorn's plants are slow growing, tenacious, and thrive in shade, and their colors are dark and muted greens, rich browns, and ghostly silvers and gray. Saturn confers medicinal properties, hardiness in cold or drought, and strong leaves and stems. Herbs, resins, oils, fruits, vegetables, woods, and flowers that strongly exhibit one or more of these qualities can be called upon to support your magic. Here are a few examples:

- Horsetail (equisetum) because it strengthens bones and the boundary of the aura.
- Mullein for communing with the dead and its healing properties.
- Skullcap for lifting moods and strengthening loyalty.
- Caraway for protection and sealing promises.
- Burdock for reversal magick and cleansing physical and energetic toxins.

Once you understand the rationale for making these assignments, the lists of correspondences will make more sense. Another thing to consider is that each part of a plant may resonate more strongly with a different element, planet, and sign. Willow (salix) shows its connection with Capricorn and Saturn with its bark's bitter taste that has medicinal qualities for pain and inflammation. However, willow is also an herb of the Moon; it loves water, is flexible, and is excellent for making wands and dowsing rods. Which energy steps forward depends on your call and invitation. "Like calls to like" is a truism in witchcraft. When you use your Capricorn nature to make a call, you are answered by the Capricorn part of the plant.

Plant materials can take the form of incense, anointing oils, altar pieces, potions, washes, magickal implements, foods, flower arrangements, and so on. The mere presence of plant material that is linked to Capricorn or Saturn will be helpful to you. However, to gain the most benefit from plant energy, you need to actively engage with it. Push some of your energy into the plants and then pull on it to start the flow. Although much of the plant material you work with will be dried or preserved, it retains a connection to living members of its species. You may also want to reach out and try to commune with the spirit, the group soul, of the plants to request their assistance or guidance. This will awaken the power slumbering in the dried or preserved plant material. Spending time with living plants, whether they be houseplants, in your yard, or in a public garden, will strengthen your conversation with the green beings under Capricorn's eye.

Crystals

Before digging into this topic, let's clear up some of the confusion around the birthstones for the signs of the zodiac. There are many varying lists for birthstones. Also be aware that some are related to the calendar month rather than the zodiacal signs. There are traditional lists, but the most commonly available lists for birthstones were created by jewelers to sell more jewelry. Also be cautious of the word *traditional* as some jewelers refer to the older lists compiled by jewelers as "traditional." The traditional lists created by magickal practitioners also diverge from each other because of cultural differences and the availability of different stones in the times and places the lists were created. If you have already formed a strong connection to a birthstone that you discover is not really connected to the energy of your sign, keep using it. Your connection is proof of its value to you in moving, holding, and shifting energy, whether or not it is specifically attuned to Capricorn.

These are my preferred assignments of birthstones for the signs of the zodiac:

Aries	Bloodstone, Carnelian, Diamond
Taurus	Rose Quartz, Amber, Sapphire
Gemini	Agate, Tiger's Eyes, Citrine
Cancer	Moonstone, Pearl, Emerald
Leo	Heliodor, Peridot, Black Onyx

Virgo	Green Aventurine, Moss Agate, Zircon
Libra	Jade, Lapis Lazuli, Labradorite
Scorpio	Obsidian, Pale Beryl, Nuummite
Sagittarius	Turquoise, Blue Topaz, Iolite
Capricorn	Black Tourmaline, Howlite, Ruby
Aquarius	Amethyst, Sugalite, Garnet
Pisces	Ametrine, Smoky Quartz, Aquamarine

There are many other possibilities that work just as well, and I suggest you find what responds best for you as an individual. I've included all twelve signs in case you'd like to use the stones for your Moon sign or rising sign. Hands-on experimentation is the best approach, so I suggest visiting crystal or metaphysical shops and rock and mineral shows when possible. Here's some information on the three I prefer for Capricorn.

Black Tourmaline

This trigonal crystal helps deflect and absorb negative energies and emotions from other people. It comes in many colors, but black is best for Capricorns. It also helps you work through your own anxiety and reduce the intensity of inner turmoil. It is an excellent stone to help you ground and to shield without draining yourself. Black tourmaline also helps you learn how to better raise and shape energy for spells and rituals. Black tourmaline helps guide and support spiritual evolution by revealing what we must see, whether or not we wish to be confronted. This crystal makes it easier to meditate and to fully experience guided visualizations.

Howlite

This stone helps remind you of your worth and to tone down self-criticism. It helps develop your memory and capacity of concentration. Howlite can help bring balance back when your thoughts are in a loop and overly attached to specific concerns. It helps bring context and detachment so that anger or frustration can be redirected into productive actions. In day-to-day life, this crystal can be used to alert you to real-life dangers. Howlite supports the strength in bones and connection tissues when used in healing rituals. This is one of the best stones for opening up psychism in Capricorns.

Ruby

Ruby inspires exuberant enjoyment of life, which helps a Capricorn stay grounded and have an open heart. On the physical level, it adds warmth and vitality and connects you more deeply to the wisdom of your body. This gem helps you see and understand how spiritual forces affect the material world. If you are stuck, overwhelmed, or procrastinating, ruby helps break up and remove any blockages to moving forward. This stone also offers protection, especially when paired with black tourmaline. Rubies of high clarity and quality are expensive. Thankfully, cloudy rubies that are not gem quality work just as well for these purposes.

Intuition and spiritual guidance play a part in the making of correlations and, in the case of traditional lore, the collective experience of many generations of practitioners. There is also reasoning behind how these assignments are made, and understanding the process will help you choose well. Here are some examples of this reasoning:

- Crystals assigned to Capricorn are often dark, understated. or elegant colors, and some have a subtle metallic sheen to them that is the Saturnian influence. Shungite and Apache tear are good examples of these.

- Capricorn's metal is lead, a highly toxic metal that can also act as a shield against radiation. Crystals and stones that contain lead should be used with caution. Crystals such as vanadinite and wulfenite contain lead and are compatible with Capricorn energy.

Crystals such as goldstone, carnelian, and malachite whose lore and uses are related to Capricorn or Saturn actions or topics—such as endurance, perseverance, concentration, and ambition—are recommended for Capricorn.

Crystals that are the opposite of the themes for Capricorn provide a counterbalance to an excessive manifestation of Capricorn traits. For example, citrine appears on lists of crystals for many other signs but is useful for Capricorn because it brings sunshine and hopefulness to Capricorn's cool nature.

Crystals suggested for Cancer, your opposite sign, are also useful to maintain your balance.

Working with Ritual Objects

A substantial number of traditions or schools of witchcraft use magickal tools that are consecrated to represent and hold the power of the elements. Oftentimes in these systems, there is one primary tool for each of the elements and other tools that are alternatives to these or are mixtures of elements. There are many possible combinations and reasons for why the elements are assigned to different tools in different traditions and they all work within their own context. Find and follow what works best for you. Magickal tools and ritual objects are typically cleansed, consecrated, and charged to prepare them for use. In addition to following whatever procedure you may have for preparing your tools, add in a step to incorporate your energy and identity as a Capricorn witch. This is especially productive for magickal tools and ritual objects that are connected to Earth or are used to store, direct, or focus power. By adding Capricorn energy and patterning into the preparation of your tools, you will find it easier to raise, move, and shape energy with them in your workings.

There are many magickal tools and ritual objects that do not have any attachment to specific elements. The core of your life force and magickal power springs from your Capricorn Sun. So, when you consciously join your awareness of your Capricorn core with the power flowing through the tools or objects, it increases their effectiveness. Adding your earthy energy does not make it an earth tool, it makes it a Capricorn tool tuned to you. Develop the habit of using the name Capricorn as a word of power, the glyph for Capricorn for summoning power, and the greens and earthy neutral tones of Capricorn to visualize its flow. Whether it be a pendulum, a wand, a crystal, or a chalice, your Capricorn energy will be quick to rise and answer your call.

A Charging Practice

When you consciously use your Capricorn witch energy to send power into tools, it tunes them more closely to your aura. Here's a quick method for imbuing any tool with your Capricorn energy.

1. Place the tool in front of you on a table or altar.

2. Take a breath in, imagining you are breathing in silver-gray energy, and then say "Capricorn" as you exhale. Repeat this three times.

3. Place your hands on your knees and send energy into them. In this practice, the simplest form of the Capricorn glyph is used that resembles the numbers 7 and 6.

4. Use a finger to trace a 7 on your left kneecap and a 6 on your right kneecap. Place your hands back on your knees and draw in some energy. Lift your hands and clasp them, pushing your palms together tightly.

5. Now, using a finger, trace the glyph of Capricorn over or on the tool you are charging. Repeat this several times and imagine the glyph being absorbed by the tool.

6. Pick up the tool, take in a breath while imaging silver-gray energy, then blow that charged breath over the tool.

7. Say "blessed be!" and proceed with using the tool or putting it away.

Hopefully this charging practice will inspire you and encourage you to experiment. Use the name *Capricorn* as a word of power, the glyph for Capricorn for summoning power, and the colors of Capricorn whenever possible. Feel free to use these spontaneously. Whether it be a pendulum, a wand, a crystal, a chalice, a ritual robe, or anything else that catches your imagination, these simple methods can have a large impact. The Capricorn energy you imprint into objects will be quick to rise and answer your call.

Crystal Success Spell for the Capricorn Witch

Nicholas Pearson

The steadfast, earthy nature of crystals has always felt reassuring to my Capricornian sensibilities. Crystals and gemstones have long connoted some of the same themes and aspirations of Capricorn—like ambition, status, success, and authority—and they are excellent allies for the Capricorn witch seeking to achieve the great and ambitious work associated with our natal sign. With the right mix of stones, you can support the Capricornian longing to achieve success. This spell is aimed at the big picture, helping you move toward big goals and creating a legacy that lives on beyond your everyday work.

You will need:

+ A candle whose color corresponds to your intent
+ A garnet, a citrine, and an emerald

Instructions:

Garnet, a popular birthstone for those under the sign of Capricorn, confers strength, stamina, and rootedness. Popularly used for wealth magic, this gemstone gives weight and form to ideas so they can become reality. Citrine is among the foremost of stones regarded for success and prosperity. Its golden hues offer warmth and optimism while also helping you let go of the past—qualities often needed to counteract the gravitas of Saturn. Emerald is linked to Capricorn's ruling planet in some occult teachings, and it synthesizes Saturn's best virtues, reminding you of the power and agency you have in the material world. Emerald is a light bearer that leads you toward realizing your potential and leaving your mark on the world. (I've chosen emerald for its Saturnian correspondences in certain streams of occult teachings, but you could choose another stone of Saturn, like black onyx, jet, blue sapphire, sodalite, or galena, if it should better suit your working preference.)

To perform this spell, reflect on what you'd like to pour your Capricornian magic into; it can be a concrete, short-term goal, or the bigger ambition of fulfilling your life's work. Select a candle color aligned with your intention and carve the glyph for Capricorn into the wax. Next, cleanse the three stones by whatever method you prefer. Hold them in your hands and conjure the image of your goal, directing the feelings evoked by this into the stones. Place the candle in its holder and arrange the three freshly charged gemstones in an equilateral triangle around the candle. Quiet your mind and visualize the ambition you wish to see fulfilled. Light the candle and imagine that its warmth and glow are broadcast farther by the gemstones around it; see its energy reaching out into the world. Recite the following incantation:

By gemstones three and candlelight
My ambition now is blessed
Like a torch that's shining bright
May it lead me to success.

Allow the candle to burn down, and when it's finished, place the stones in a prominent place to be reminded of their magic each day or carry them in a small pouch whenever you work toward attaining your goals. Each time you see them or feel their weight as you carry them, reflect on the meaning and magic of these gemstones and know that you are one step closer to realizing your ambitions each day.

HERBAL
CORRESPONDENCES

♑

These plant materials all have a special connection to your energy as a Capricorn witch. There are many more, but these are a good starting point.

Herbs	
Comfrey	to protect travelers and set boundaries
Burdock	clarifies wishes and intentions
Wintergreen	cleanses and draws in positive energy

Flowers

Petunia	for acknowledging and releasing dark emotions
Hellebore	clarity of thought and banishing spirits
Pansy	for love, calling rain, and restoring peace

Incense and Fragrances

Ambrette Seeds	stirs passions and determination
Patchouli	for luck and money
Vetiver	for comfort, stability, renewed focus

CLEANSING AND SHIELDING

Maria Wander

The most magical tool of the Capricorn witch is the witch themselves. Before starting off on any type of magical shielding, prepare by being grounded, centered, and focused on the work at hand. Creating a shield can prevent toxic energies from coming in, and they can also prevent toxic energies from exiting as you would want them to. Ideally you will want to cleanse first before shielding. So let's start with a couple of easy cleansing techniques.

Spiritual Bath and Auric Blade Cleansing Practice

The simplest way to cleanse your energetic field and physical body is by washing with salt water, envisioning the ionic release of negativity from your energy, and using your hands like an auric squeegee blade to remove any residue. Salt and herbs are effective ingredients that release undesirable detritus lingering on your energy body.

You will need:

+ 1 cup salt (sea salt, Epsom salt, kosher salt, or pink Himalayan salt preferred)
+ ¼ cup baking soda
+ ¼ cup Saturn herbs (horsetail, nettle, and comfrey) (optional)
+ 3 drops each horsetail, nettle, and comfrey essential oils (optional)
+ Towel

Instructions:

Mix the salt with the baking soda for the most basic spiritual bath to cleanse with. Add the optional herbs and oils, if using.

Place into a bath and soak for fifteen to twenty minutes while envisioning the ionic release of negativity from your energy. If you prefer showering, place the bath components into a basin of water and stir until well dissolved. After showering as you usually would, pour the basin of water up over yourself from head to toe while envisioning the ionic release of negativity from your energy.

Dry yourself, step from the bath, and rub your palms together in a circular motion.

Use your hands as an auric blade, starting from your head downward, sweeping any energetic detritus into the scooped palms of your hands. Envision the ionic release. Sweep hands from crown past your face to neck and flick into the water or shower stall. Repeat, passing your hands down from your crown past your ears and flick again. Next, pass your hands down from your crown behind your head to your neck, and flick. Continue for the remainder of your torso, energetically extending your reach to the part of your back you cannot physically sweep. Blade-cleanse legs and feet. Flick after each pass.

A spiritual spray can be a quick fix for when you don't have a bathroom handy. Place Florida Water in a clean spray bottle and spray yourself from the top of your head downward, then follow the remaining steps as described.

Cleansing Your Space

Our living and working spaces need help to refresh their surroundings as energy can get stagnant, like a smelly pond. Spending time in yucky places can affect our moods and our own energy, too. One method uses sound vibrations to clear out old energy. Use a brass bell and ring it in the center of the room, then move to ring it in each corner of the room. This will dislodge and clear any negativity after there has been an argument or sharp words spoken in a room. Vibration is an effective form of energetic cleansing as the resonance continues past the sound that can be heard.

Cinnamon sticks are also ideal for space cleansing as they can be set on fire and placed in a firesafe bowl to keep burning embers secure. Cense each room and open the front door to let out any energy from the past inhabitants or visitors. If you have a cinnamon broom, sweep the energy from each room. Place a cinnamon stick on the lintel above any doorway used to enter or exit the home as protection and to attract abundance and good fortune.

To shield each doorway and window, rub both hands together until your palms warm, then scribe an energetic invoking earth pentacle:

+ Extend from the topmost point of the star down to the left knee
+ Up to the right shoulder, across to the left shoulder

+ Down to the right knee and back up to the starting point

State this as you scribe each pentacle: "Away evil spirits.
What enters and exits here is by my will alone."

Shielding Methods

After cleansing yourself, your aura, and your space, it's always
a good idea to shield. This keeps negative energy from accu-
mulating in the first place, particularly if you do it often.

The pentacle shield is effective to protect both you and
your home. Renew the shield every week on Saturday, ideally
at Saturn hour. Here's how to do it:

+ Scribe an energetic circle on the ground in front
  of you. Quarter the circle with two lines to create
  the equal-arm cross that is the glyph of the Earth.
+ Rub both hands together until your palms are
  warm, then scribe a second circle over top of the
  first. Scribe an invoking pentacle of earth within it.
+ Open the palm of your dominant hand over the
  circle. Pull the circle up energetically like a column
  to knee level and step inside of it. Continue to pull
  up the column energetically above your head. Clap
  your hands above your head to complete the shield.
+ State, "My shield defends, it shields from harm,
  my shield protects, my shield alarms."

+ Energetically expand the pentacle column all
  about you to your desired size, perhaps the size
  of the room, your house, the block you live on.
  When you are satisfied with the boundary, envision the sickle-shaped glyph of Saturn at your
  third eye, breathe in slowly, and breathe out even
  more slowly through your mouth to lock in the
  new limits you have set.

Another shield to try is the bubble shield. Bubble shields
use your personal etheric energy to make and keep running.
They are helpful to moderate everyday empathic concerns to
keep energy steady and protected from psychic leeching. I have
used them as a New York City nurse in the emergency department and when attending rock and crystal shows where con-
centrated energies vibrate. Start by placing your thumbs at
your navel and hands two inches below your navel. Stamp your
feet to awaken the energy points on your soles and communicate with the earth. Breathe in and out while concentrating on
your center. Straighten out your posture as if a golden thread
is attached to the crown of your head, lengthening your spine,
that golden thread shooting out into the sky, connecting to
the cosmos. Take another breath in and out and when you are
ready, push any negativity you may be experiencing out from
your solar plexus. See a flash of golden glow from the center of
your torso shine forth above your navel.

Next, visualize a bubble forming around your entire body. As it takes energetic form, see a flash of iridescent rainbow reflecting off the bubble. Energize it so that it remains semiporous, allowing communications and positivity to flow in and out, yet keeping unwanted emotions from entering. Every few hours, breathe energy into the bubble to sustain it. When you no longer need the bubble, simply pop it with your thoughts and it will dissipate.

Flower and Gem Empowered

Crystal, stone, and gem magic can strongly impact us because of our affinity to Earth. Here are some energetic precautionary measures and subtle vibrational energy medicine practices on flower and gem essences that are helpful to know.

Flower essences are a specific type of herbal healing using the energetic vibration of flowers as complementary, alternative medicine. These liquid plant preparations can be ingested to bolster immunity, improve mood, boost confidence, reinforce boundaries, process grief, and support emotional well-being. Flower essences can be purchased or homemade to work on the subtle emotional body and rework concerns related to long-standing patterns needing insight and resolution. They can both help cleanse your aura or shield your energy, depending on the flowers you select.

Making Flower Essences

Satisfy your earthiness by making essences with plants you have a real connection with. Note that this must be done on a sunny day as you'll be using freshly picked flowers, no cut or dried flowers. Only make flower essences when you're 100 percent certain what the flower is and that it is safe for consumption and free from herbicide.

You will need:
+ A medium-size glass bowl
+ Spring water (8 ounces)
+ A handful of freshly picked flowers
+ A clean glass canning jar (16 ounce/pint size)
+ Wooden chopsticks
+ 80-proof alcohol (8 ounces) such as vodka or brandy (do not use rubbing alcohol)
+ A 2-ounce dropper bottle

Instructions:
Before making your own flower essences, connect with your flower. Meditate near it and thank the flower for sharing with you. Ask for blooms to create energy medicine with. Check for an energetic yes or no. I usually sing my thanks to the flower at the moment I receive a

yes answer to ensure that there has been an energetic exchange. Snip blooms directly into the bowl and fill with spring water without causing any shadows to cross over the water. Allow the bowl to sit in sunlight for three or more hours.

Use wooden chopsticks to remove flowers from the water and compost them. Pour the water in a clean glass canning jar and add an equal amount of 80-proof alcohol to create a 50:50 dilution called the mother essence. It will last for about a year. Alcohol can be replaced with vinegar or glycerin, and these should be kept for six months refrigerated.

To make what is called a daughter essence, add ten drops of mother to a two-ounce dropper bottle and fill the remainder, half with spring water, half with 80-proof alcohol. Again, alcohol can be replaced with vinegar or glycerin.

Take four drops of the daughter essence four times a day dropped onto your tongue or into water to drink. Place the essence into a spray bottle as a mist to chill your face and shoulders, soles of your feet, your workspace, inside your car, or your sheets and pillows.

Here are some flower essences that can be made using familiar flowers:

+ Daisy flower essence connects our hearts and
  our minds to bring clarity to intuition and
  alignment with the higher Self.
+ Dandelion flower essence is energizing,
  grounding, calming, focusing, helps you
  express your life force dynamically, and
  brings awareness to better identify emotions
  that result in underlying tension.
+ Plantain flower essence releases negative
  thought patterns, mental blocks, resent-
  ments, and grief, which can weigh down
  the lungs and respiratory system.
+ Mugwort flower essence helps with overwhelm, provides balance and grounding,
  and promotes visualization and insightful
  dreams.

Make crystal essences with a similar method. Choose
a crystal whose energy you want to partake in, whether
that's for cleansing, shielding, or tuning in to your Capricorn energy, like black tourmaline. You can use any stone
since it will not be coming in direct contact with the water
you'll be ingesting.

First, clear the crystal by placing it on a selenite slab if water soluble or by pouring spring water over it for one minute. Next, hold the crystal in the palm of your hand and connect with it, communicating your intent. Place the crystal in a glass small enough to fit in a glass bowl filled with spring water. State your intent for the crystal essence and charge under the sunlight or the moonlight for three or more hours. Follow the steps to complete the gem elixir. You do not need to make separate mother/daughter essences. Gem elixirs can be used to anchor the energetic changes obtained from using flower essences as stones contain ancient devas of many years' wisdom. Their vibrations stabilize and protect our energy bodies to maintain balance during the expansion of consciousness.

Anchorstones: A Travel Charm for Homebodies

M. Belanger

Ambitious goats often find ourselves in jobs requiring travel—but what do you do when you're a fussy Capricorn who has trouble feeling comfortable in new places? Bring a little piece of home with you! This is a homebrew spell I use to help make unfamiliar spaces a little more comfortable.

You will need:

* Two similar stones, crystals, or other small objects that fit easily into the palm of your hand
* A small corner of your living space
* A personalized sigil (optional)

Instructions:

This charm is as much a practice as it is a spell (perfect if you're a creature of habit) and it speaks to our earthy groundedness in familiar things.

First, select two small items. I use polished river stones for their smoothness, heft, and how easy it is to paint on them. You might choose crystals, beads, acorns, driftwood, or something else. The nature of the objects is up to you: first and foremost, they should appeal to your sensitivities so you can effectively build a connection with these two items. They also need to be easily portable and look reasonably similar, if not identical.

Next, set a small space aside in your home. This can be a countertop, a bookshelf, the top of a dresser—ideally, it will be a location you pass regularly during the course of your day; some part of your space you associate with comfort, familiarity, and *home*. You can make this into a full-blown altar to your household spirits if you like, or it can simply be a little bowl or plate where only these two objects live.

The key is to establish the anchorstones as a part of your home. Let them soak up the energy, and each time you pass them, take a moment to notice them so you build a strong association between their presence and everything you find comfortable about your space.

When you must travel, take one and leave one. With the link built between them, when you touch the stone traveling with you, you will resonate with the comfortable space where its partner still resides.

As an optional act of magic, develop a sigil that means "home" to you and paint, carve, or otherwise inscribe this upon these anchorstones. Each should bear this sigil and it will help maintain their link both to one another and to the comfort of your space.

Additional Tips

When traveling, in addition to your anchorstone, take several familiar things that speak to your senses: A scent you associate with home. A blanket or piece of clothing whose texture comforts you. Small nibbles of foods you deeply enjoy that you might not be able to get on the road. While it's impractical to pack *everything* that reminds you of home, adding a few elements that ground you in the sensory associations of your comfortable space can really help.

WHAT SETS A CAPRICORN OFF, AND HOW TO RECOVER

Maria Wander

What plucks on the last nerve of a Capricorn witch is when a concern is allowed to fester, stew, and then develops into a full-blown crisis everyone complains of, but no one you know actually does anything about it. Even when something gets my goat, I strive to look for the opportunity that comes along with the obstacle. This is a tried-and-true Capricorn formula for counteracting irritants, complications, and naysayers.

Don't Get Angry, Get Active

Take for example the global colony collapse disorder of worker bees affecting honeybee colonies. My heart aches for these hardworking, community-focused little bumbles. Shrinking habitats and pesticide use hinder their flight and ability to pollinate. As their number dwindles, they leave behind food stores of honey and pollen with queens unattended and capped broods abandoned in hives. So many wild bees have died, needful crop pollination has led to commercial beekeeping becoming a billion-dollar industry. In the United States, they are trucked state to state, one truck for 22 million bees; that's 400 hives, each with 50,000 honeybees. Bees thrive best in a biodiverse landscape, so large-scale monoculture results in their high mortality rate. The more I learned, the more I knew I had to do something, despite cynics and doubters.

To combat this on a personal scale, I trained to be a beekeeper. I started study in classes, gradually expanding to take part in community programs. I kept hives on my NYC patio near the million plus plants at the Botanical Gardens. Once the colonies split, I took them to my family out in the suburbs. While bee losses continue, other likeminded souls taking action has led to a 500 percent increase in active beehives in New York City, with all beekeepers now required to register annually.

When a situation is brewing that gets our hackles up, rather than getting entrenched in anger, we change the pattern by considering other possibilities and pitching in. Saturn gifts obstacles as teachers and lessons. When Capricorn is set off in anger or annoyance, it signals us to action. The planet Mars is exalted in Capricorn after all, and

Capricorn as a cardinal sign is associated with beginnings, the start of the season, with the power to awaken and renew. We are the "no ifs, ands, or buts" brigade. Rather than getting locked into a mindset or waiting to see if something can be done, we shift and consider what to do or how. This swings us subtly from being on the back foot to placing a firm step forward, redirecting wrath, ready to initiate and push ahead.

For instance, some Capricorn neighborhood witches banded a fellowship together to celebrate holidays and do witchy things on a regular monthly basis. While out on a few fun jaunts, just how trashy the roadways had gotten became a topic of heated conversation. Litter around the roadside was a terrible eyesore but also a safety hazard, an environmental issue, and a health hazard. Exasperated by the litter strewn about the neighborhood, the discussion shifted from angry irritation about what was wrong to hopeful planning to make things right. This became one of the best scheduled gatherings: the day-long litter pickup Keep It Clean events. In taking ownership of matters and creating local cleanup meets, the outcome was a successful clearing up of the streets, protection of the environment, engagement in community service, and maintenance of order.

Mitigating Challenges

Another thing that ignites Capricorn fury is when we aren't accorded our due since we strive to do the best for ourselves and others. While the daunting challenges of the worldwide pandemic have left no one untouched, how nurses and health caregivers were publicly applauded but privately undervalued really riled me. Burnout, lack of support, and pay incommensurate with duties have triggered a critical shortage. More than 200,000 new nurses are needed annually to meet the rise in chronic conditions, a sizeable aging population, staff retirement, and faculty shortages that constrain the creation of future professionals. What can one do in the face of all this? Channel ire toward outcome.

After an eighteen-month grind to attain partial grant financing, I went back to school and obtained a doctorate. I began teaching at university, training new nurses, and conducting nonprofit healthcare projects to support subsidized funding for programs I took part in to enhance recruitment, retention, staff autonomy, engagement, and satisfaction. I get to teach each nurse who comes into the medical center where I work and precept students in residencies and capstones. I can't solve the staffing shortage myself, but it takes the edge off to support and enhance the profession doing what I can, how I can, to the best of my ability. To my nursing sisters, brethren, and health workers meeting the same challenges, who go back to it all again after sparse rest, you are true s/heroes.

Now if you're so angered and disappointed by betrayal or disrespect that you can't just let go, then let it rip. By that I mean engage in scream or projectile therapy. Express your angst and your stress; get it out of you before it takes purchase and burrows deep. For scream therapy, place your face in a pillow and yell to unbottle it all. If you need to have words with someone but are too angry to get them out without losing control, take a shower, and while there, practice your side of the argument in an imaginary conversation with the other. Yell and let the anger get out of you and down the drain. For projectile therapy, find somewhere safe where you can pitch ice cubes and let them fly without injury to self or others or throw eggs. Eggs have a material potentiality in them, which will take in negative energy and draw it from you. Yell your fury into the egg and give it a hurl against a surface.

Transmuting Rudeness

Other pet peeves of any Capricorn are the rise in rudeness from random strangers, time wasted, and those who sneer or mock our worker ant tendencies. You may have noted the former when online or at a coffee line or a checkout counter. For the latter, it's not that Caps don't relax; we do take time to wind down and to revel, but we do it like it's our job. On my subway commute, I usually do handcrafts as a meditative, therapeutic practice. During one trip, I was double knitting socks, one inside another in a simultaneous pair, a technical challenge and tactile joy. The person sitting opposite watched first with curious interest, then appalled aversion. Disdainfully they commented, "You know, you can just buy a pack of socks for a few bucks at [insert name of big box store] to wear every day." When I didn't immediately reply, they spoke louder: "Why bother doing all of that work?"

Now, handcrafted socks are delightful to wear and make. No bothersome seams, and when wool fibers are used, they wick moisture and keep your feet comfy and cozy during all seasons. I knit with purpose and magic. Socks in particular are worked well using this chant: "Empower my steps to guide me true on the path of my natal promise." I took a breath before replying with a smile to the doubter in a calm, steely tone, "Why such a critic? Would you prefer custom and bespoke, or made for the masses? I can show you how knitting both these socks together is done." They were surprised I'd answered their churlishness with a measure of friendly polite inquiry. It took the wind out of their sails, and they said no to end the exchange.

When someone is tactless, nasty, or uncivil and ticks you off, first take a beat. Relax your jaw and pause before firing back at them with the same venom or escalating. Use a question to call them on their behavior, show it is inappropriate. You next might also consider how to make the exchange a productive one or to distract and focus their attention elsewhere with humor to disrupt any tension between you. If you go for a laugh, make sure you're both in on the joke; humor that is one sided and mean spirited won't cut it. Don't let your irritation with the offensive annoyer turn you into one. Human conflict is inevitable. Managing our anger from within and facing external conflict with aplomb sets boundaries for those involved; it can create connection and get our point across in a way that shifts angst so it doesn't live in you rent free.

Afterward, I reflected on the passing disparagement as either a mean attempt on their part to boost sense of self at a stranger's expense or a microaggression—maybe a bit of both. Without getting to know them better, I'd never find out—and didn't need to. The brief interchange had bugged me, but then comparing it to what is of real importance, I shrugged off the last remaining bit of pique so it wouldn't infect the rest of day. Rudeness is contagious. When on the receiving end, give the benefit of the doubt but hold your corner; avoid responding to unpleasant disrespect with similar offense or holding a grudge just to pass along to some other unsuspecting stranger. Transmute negativity into self-awareness and compassion, like the witch you are. Change what you can, let go of the rest.

A BRIEF BIO OF DOREEN VALIENTE

* * *

Jason Mankey

There are very few people who have had a bigger impact on modern witchcraft than Doreen Valiente. If you've ever danced *The Witches' Rune* or read *The Charge of the Goddess*, you've experienced the words and magick of Doreen Valiente (nee Dominy). Hailed by many as the mother of modern witchcraft, Valiente's contributions to the Craft are immense, and it's not hyperbole to suggest that modern witchcraft would look very different today without Doreen.

Valiente was born in southeast London (Surrey) in 1922 on January 4. During World War II, Doreen worked as a translator and for the United Kingdom's intelligence service at Benchley Park in London. While working for the British government, Doreen met Casimiro Valiente (1918–1971), a Spanish immigrant who had fought in that country's civil war. The two were married in 1944, with Doreen taking Casimiro's last name.

Doreen had become interested in magick and the occult at a young age; she cast her first spell at age thirteen, and by the late 1940s had begun practicing ceremonial magick. In 1952 she met Gerald Gardner (the world's first modern public witch and the architect of what is now known as Wicca) and was initiated into the Craft by him at the summer solstice in 1953.

After initiation, Valiente began revising many of the rituals in Gardner's book of shadows along with adding new ones. Valiente's time working with Gardner was transformative, but also quite brief, and by 1957 she and Gardner had a falling out over the latter's love of publicity.

In 1962 Valiente published her first book, *Where Witchcraft Lives*, which examined the history of witchcraft in Sussex, England. Two years later she began working with Robert Cochrane (born Roy Bowers, 1931–1966), one of the first public practitioners of "traditional witchcraft." That same year at dinner held by the Witchcraft Research Association, Valiente became the first person to ever publicly mention the *Wiccan Rede* ("an' it harm none do what you will").

By the mid 1960s, Valiente had emerged as one of English witchcraft's primary spokespeople, and during the 1970s became one of contemporary witchcraft's most important (and gifted) writers. Her 1978 book *Witchcraft for Tomorrow* is especially notable for its embrace of solitary practitioners and initiations beyond the then-conventional coven structure. Valientes's 1989 memoir *The Rebirth of Witchcraft* remains required reading for anyone interested in the history of the Craft. She passed away in September of 1999 from pancreatic cancer.

Valiente spent most of her adult life in Brighton, England, never quite grasping just how influential she had become among witches. Valiente believed the Craft was for everyone and was one of the first well-known witches to publicly advocate for gay rights. In 2013, a blue plaque was unveiled in her honor at Tyson Place, the council flat she called home for nearly thirty years, commemorating her contributions to English society.

A Sampling of Capricorn Occultists

GAVIN BONE
author, witch, organizer, and teacher
(January 19, 1964)

PETER JAMES CARROLL
author, occultist, chaos magic theorist
(January 8, 1953)

DOROTHY CLUTTERBUCK
primary source for creation of Wicca
(January 19, 1880)

SABINA MAGLIOCCO
witch, author, and professor of anthropology
(December 30, 1959)

MARIAN GREEN
author on witchcraft and the Western Mysteries
(January 1, 1944)

MONICA SJÖÖ
artist, author, and radical anarcho-/ecofeminist
(December 31, 1938)

THE SWAY OF YOUR MOON SIGN

Ivo Dominguez, Jr.

The Moon is the reservoir of your emotions, thoughts, and all your experiences. The Moon guides your subconscious, your unconscious, and your instinctive response in the moment. The Moon serves as the author, narrator, and musical score in the ongoing movie in your mind that summarizes and mythologizes your story. The Moon is like a scrying mirror, a sacred well, that gives answers to the question of the meaning of your life. The style and the perspective of your Moon sign shapes your story, a story that starts as a reflection of your Sun sign's impetus. The remembrance of your life events is a condensed subjective story, and it is your Moon sign that summarizes and categorizes the data stream of your life.

In witchcraft, the Moon is our connection and guide to the physical and energetic tides in nature, the astral plane, and other realities. The Moon in the heavens as it moves through signs and phases also pulls and pushes on your aura. The Moon in your birth chart reveals the intrinsic qualities and patterns in your aura, which affects the form your magick takes. Your Sun sign may be the source of your essence and power, but your Moon sign shows how you use that power in your magick. This chapter describes the twelve possible arrangements of Moon signs with a Capricorn Sun and what each combination yields.

Moon in Aries

Capricorn likes to plan everything, and an Aries Moon prefers to be impulsive, which creates some inner friction. Both signs are driven by their goals, but the Aries Moon adds a more competitive spirit. An Aries Moon gives you the glow of confidence and the dynamism that marks a natural leader. It is easier for you to collect friends, allies, and followers.

You don't ever want to admit defeat or backtrack to start over. When you regularly compromise and adapt to your circumstances rather than fighting every step, you'll reach more of your goals. The arts of diplomacy don't come naturally to you but are worth the effort to learn. You are good at spotting deception or questionable motives. You often feel called to enforce your brand of justice; ask yourself if it is truly your job to do so.

You are more passionate than most Capricorns, but you still have much of the control and reserve that are common to your sign. You tend to be skeptical of people who show their cards or wear their hearts on their sleeve. Try to give people who are gushing sweetness and positivity a chance; some of them are authentic. Moreover, you need a counterbalancing influence to your saturnine and martial nature. Your friends and romantic partners need to know that you still care about them when you get lost in your work and projects. Schedule shows of affection and kindness; relationships are work and require your attention. You don't like being bored and your idea of recreation does not include much in the way of rest. At the very least, make sure you keep a regular sleep cycle for your health's sake.

An Aries Moon, like all the fire element Moons, easily stretches forth to connect with the energy of other beings. Your fiery qualities cleanse and protect your aura from picking up other people's emotional debris or being influenced by your environment. It is relatively easy for you to blend your energy with others and to separate cleanly. However, take care not to use up too much of your own energy or exhaust yourself. The energy field and magic of an Aries Moon tends to move and change faster than any other sign, but it is harder to hold to a specific task or shape. This can be overcome with self-awareness and practice. Magick related to increasing vitality, protection, success, and banishing negativity comes easily to you.

Moon in Taurus

Both your Sun and your Moon are in the element of earth, which gives you a grounded, dependable, and resolute nature. Generally, you are calm and levelheaded, but you are also more rigid and less compromising with this combination. You enjoy the pleasures of the world and the company of people more than most Capricorns. You tend to be nostalgic, retro, or conservative in your tastes for yourself. However, you attract many different types of friends and colleagues because of your loyal and straightforward nature. When you say you are a friend, you truly mean it. Some might say you are an old soul, but it is truer to say that your maturity comes from paying attention to what you experience in the world and learning from it.

This Moon encourages you to stop and smell the roses, to enjoy the world. Allow yourself to revel in your Moon's Taurean sensuality. However, avoid excess, or you'll become self-critical if you fall behind on your goals. Procrastination is a big warning sign that you need to recharge your connection to the things that bring you joy and purpose. In astrology, the Moon is said to be exalted in Taurus, which means that it favors success. Taurus is ruled by Venus, so you tend to have more emotional intelligence than most Capricorns. This will serve you at home and work. Creating experiences that you can share with others is the best medicine for you when you are feeling stuck in your life. You want things to be straightforward and uncomplicated in all arenas of your life.

A Taurus Moon generates an aura that is magnetic and pulls energy inward. You are good at raising energy for yourself and others in workings and rituals. This Moon also makes it easier to create strong shields and wards. If something does manage to breach your shields or create some other type of energetic injury, get some healing help so that the problem resolves faster. Generally, people with a Taurus Moon have less flexibility in their aura. You can work toward improving your flexibility, but the quick fix is to create new boundaries or a larger container. Astral travel and other forms of soul travel are harder to learn with this Moon sign, but you have a gift for merging and communicating with spirits of place or land spirits. Spells for abundance, fertility, animal communication, and safety come easily to you.

♊

Moon in Gemini

Your Capricorn's drive makes your Gemini Moon's curiosity stronger so you are always learning something new. Over time you will become competent in many things and can be an expert when you apply yourself. These two signs complement each other, filling in the gaps in aptitudes. Gemini's versatility joined with Capricorn's decisiveness and willpower is hard to beat. This combination gives you many career and interest options. Gemini gives you more adaptability than most Capricorns so you can chameleon yourself into many social or work settings. You do need to learn patience as no amount of effort or desire will overturn the rules of the Earth plane. The good news is you always have backup plans, side hustles, or side adventures to entertain you as longer-term projects slowly mature.

You are good at rationalizing things or being stoic to manage discomforts, but some type of meditation or relaxation process would be a helpful addition to your practices. Find the time to be outdoors in nature as this will make you more grounded. This combination tends to make you more interested in companionship than romance. You are a good talker and know how to be charming, so attracting people is not a problem. You like the idea of working and playing together with common goals. There are people you may wish to keep in your life who need romance; you can learn to do this. Your to-do list for your life is long and giving more attention to your body and health will make it possible to check more items off the list. Your Capricorn Sun cares about longevity, but your Gemini Moon needs reminders.

A Gemini Moon, like all the air Moons, makes it easier to engage in soul travel and psychism and gives the aura greater flexibility. When an air type aura reaches out and touches something, it can quickly read and copy the patterns it finds. A Gemini Moon gives the capacity to quickly adapt and respond to changing energy conditions in working magick or using the psychic senses. However, turbulent spiritual atmospheres are felt strongly and can be uncomfortable or cause harm. A wind can pick up and carry dust and debris and the same is true for an aura. If you need to cleanse your energy, become still and the debris will simply fall out of your aura. Magick that arises from the spoken or written word is strong in you. There is a special gift for sigil magick.

Moon in Cancer

A Cancer Moon means you are more in touch with your feelings than most Capricorns. Cancer is also the sign opposite to Capricorn, which gives you inner tension and more complexity of character. This combination can produce a consciousness that joins emotional intelligence with practical thought to produce wisdom and shrewd choices. You have worldly ambitions but also a great need for a safe home and hearth. You also have a need for a close circle of family or friends to feel secure in your life. The Cancer Moon gives you a desire to protect and take care of those you like or love. Often this combination comes with difficult circumstances, especially early in life, that make it harder to open your heart. Cynicism may feel protective but is corrosive and leads you astray. It's reasonable to have a tough and nonchalant persona as your armor in the world, but make sure you let your tenderness show too. Otherwise, you'll miss out on important people and opportunities.

Both Capricorn and Cancer are prone to being their own worst critic. This can develop into a feedback loop. Be mindful of this so you can interrupt a pattern that is hurtful and unproductive. When you trust your capabilities and your intuition, you are perceptive and persuasive and come up with the best plans and ideas. Step up and show the world what you have to offer. Friends and partners who are nurturing and supportive of your true self are what you need; accept nothing less. You may have a delicate digestion, or some other physical indicator, when you are stressed. Your feelings turn into physical sensations easily. Turn this to your advantage by heeding the warning early and taking care of yourself. This will let you live a longer and healthier life.

A Cancer Moon, like all the water Moons, gives the aura a magnetic pull that wants to merge with whatever is nearby. Imagine two drops of water growing closer until they barely touch and how they pull together to become one larger drop. The aura of a person with a Cancer Moon is more likely to retain the patterns and energies it touches. You must take extra care to cleanse and purify yourself before and after magickal work whenever possible. One of the gifts that comes with this Moon is a capacity for offering good counsel, helping people in states of transition, and divination in all its forms.

Moon in Leo

This fiery Moon makes for a more self-assured version of Capricorn. These two signs together increase your charisma, need for success, and time in the spotlight. This Moon increases your optimism and comfort in taking risks, which lets you get started faster in achieving your goals. When you encounter obstacles on your path, you become colder and more cunning. Sometimes this is the right course of action, but at other times the long-term consequences may not be acceptable. You are proud and dignified, which can lead to staying true to your ideals or to being arrogant and cruel. If you live your life in an exemplary way rather than as a cautionary tale, you will have greater joy and recognition. When you stay grounded and centered, you are a force of nature, skilled and precise in all your actions. You will be remembered, and you leave a lasting mark in the world.

When it comes to friends and loved ones, you need to develop a different set of skills and behaviors. You will have no trouble attracting people, but to get the ones you want to keep close to your heart, you need to offer praise and admiration. They need personal autonomy as much as you do, and they have their own dreams. You can be really good at discovering what others need to feel cared for and it feeds your soul to provide it. The more you help them grow, the happier everyone will be. As you get older, it seems like there is less time available to connect with people. This is not the case; you just need to reprioritize your schedule.

A Leo Moon, like all the fire element Moons, easily stretches forth to connect with the energy of other beings. The fiery qualities cleanse and protect your aura from picking up other people's emotional debris or being influenced by your environment. It is relatively easy for you to blend your energy with others and to separate cleanly. The Leo Moon also makes it easier for you to focus your power. The fixed fire of Leo makes it easier to hold large amounts of energy that can be applied for individual and collective workings. You are particularly well suited to ritual leadership or at the role of being the primary shaper of energy in a working. This combination grants special insights and skills for making magickal tools, charms, and spell pouches. You also may have a gift for oracular work or divine embodiment.

Moon in Virgo

Being a double earth sign produces a strong desire to be known for your achievements and status. You love to think, study, analyze, and juggle all the details. Internally, you are reviewing and rating everything in the world around you. You can be cold and calculating and can remain unaffected by emotional pleas or difficult situations. You have a strong sense of right and wrong as well. This Moon makes you dream of a better world and strategize on how to get there. You have high expectations for yourself and other people. This can push you to reach your potential or lock you up in hurtful self-criticism. Accept the imperfections in yourself and the world and you'll be happier and make more progress. This is part of the process of assessment and analysis and does not mean you are settling for less. It is an important step in creating an effective plan of action.

Though you gain much of your satisfaction in life from the work you do, you do need a few people you can count on. You tend not to be initially romantic, but you are loyal and drawn to interesting people. Your friendships and relationships need orderliness, harmony, reciprocity, and matching love languages. Despite outward appearances, you are very tender. You have a very refined sense of aesthetics that you apply to your clothing, décor, music, and all parts of your life. Nesting, decluttering, or reorganizing your home is a great way to relax. Working with houseplants or in a garden help your mood and health. You need more peace and quiet than most other Capricorns. Rest is not weakness, it is self-improvement. Make sure you recharge enough so that you can tackle all your projects.

A Virgo Moon, like all the earth element Moons, generates an aura that is magnetic and pulls energy inward. This Moon also makes it easier to create strong thoughtforms and energy constructs. Virgo Moons are best at perceiving and understanding patterns and process in auras, energy, spells, and so on. You can be quite good at spotting what is off and finding a way to remedy the situation. This gives the potential to do healing work and break curses among other things. The doubled earth of Capricorn Sun and Virgo Moon makes it easier to work with crystals, plant materials, and spirits of place. A knack for interpreting other people's dreams and visions often comes with this combination.

♎

Moon in Libra

You have a keen capacity for finding joy and beauty in life and this drives you almost as much as your work and desire for recognition. You are more social than most others of your sign and focus more of your energy on people. Your positive stance on the world is not always realistic, more aspirational, but this allows you to better the world by trying to make the ideal into the real. You are likely to take more risks than the average Capricorn because you believe in your competence. This combination makes you less suspicious and more comfortable in your own skin than most Capricorns. Work on developing more self-confidence and assertiveness as this Moon can make you worry too much about other people's opinions.

You are selective in who you bring into your life as you can be too trusting. For you, romance and friendships often begin through mental pursuits, or a shared affection of specific types of art, music, media, and so on. You also are more comfortable having people close who have orderly and stable lives. You give off an elegant air that can be confused with being aloof. Make sure you let people know how you feel. The incongruities between how Capricorn and Libra communicate their feelings may confuse others. Your Libra Moon craves a harmonious environment, and your Capricorn Sun helps manage your life to fill those needs. Reciprocity and a balance of give-and-take is important to you in all settings both personal and professional. This may lead to an interest in the law, politics, sociology, or humanitarian matters. Creative ventures or hobbies are the best way to keep your head and heart clear and balanced.

A Libra Moon, like all the air Moons, makes it easier to engage in soul travel and psychism and gives the aura greater flexibility. You can make yourself a neutral and clear channel for information from spirits and other entities. You are also able to tune in to unspoken requests when doing divinatory work. The auras of people with Libra Moon are very capable at bridging and equalizing differences between the subtle bodies of groups of people. This allows you to bring order and harmony to energies raised and shaped in a group ritual. You may have a talent for bargaining with spirits and placating disgruntled spirits of place or hauntings. This combination excels at using poppets, altars, knotwork, or other workings that use a proxy or symbolic link.

Moon in Scorpio

This makes for a more passionate nature than most Capricorns. This combination produces a strong competitive drive to excel. You pride yourself on your sharp intellect that catches every detail and is precise and methodical. You think of yourself as highly rational, and this is half true. You have a great deal of intuition as well. You are at your best when you honor and use your mind and your psychism. Your insight and problem-solving skills are strong, which gives the option of a wide range of careers. You have strong principles and a strong survival instinct, so you are always working to find the right balance between the two. You don't flinch when it comes to looking at the good and the bad in the world. Which is why you learn from your mistakes quickly. This Moon sign makes for the most determined and persistent of Capricorns.

Winning an argument with logic and carefully chosen phrases doesn't always lead to a rewarding outcome. Work on becoming more flexible as making room for other opinions does not weaken your own. Moreover, your natural tendency is to keep too many secrets. In general, you do not share enough, which can lead to confusion or heartache. When you do commit to a friendship or to a partner, you do so fully. The people closest to you must be able to give of themselves just as fully. Don't give up on deep intimacy as there are people out there who can match you, but it will take time to find them. If you spend enough time sorting through your thoughts and feelings, you will find your way to live your life full. To do this, you will need to work on making time for work and a personal life.

A Scorpio Moon, like all the water Moons, gives the aura a magnetic pull that wants to merge with whatever is nearby. You easily absorb information about other people, spirits, places, and so on. If you are not careful, the information and emotions will loop and repeat in your mind. To release what you have picked up, acknowledge what you perceive and then reframe its meaning in your own words. The energy and magick of a Scorpio Moon are adept at probing and moving past barriers, shields, and wards.

This also gives you the power to remove things that should not be present. This combination gives you skill in psychic magick, hypnosis, trance work, and contacting other planes of reality.

Moon in Sagittarius

You are less predictable than most other Capricorns and enthusiastic about many interests. You are outspoken and very expressive. Your fiery Moon and your earthy Sun are very different from each other and the range of attitudes and behaviors you express is very wide. However, this Moon spurs you on with a love of exploration, discovery, and constant learning. You have a great deal of charisma and an excellent sense of humor, which makes you a natural at influencing others. You have the capacity to develop strong people skills and technical skills in many fields. Some with this combination enjoy performing in front of people if they lean into their Sagittarius Moon. This blend can also lead toward humanitarian, environmental, and political work as Sagittarius inspires work for the community and Capricorn is pragmatic. Generally, you are more progressive and less bound by tradition than most others of your sign.

Sometimes this Moon encourages you to act before you have fully surveyed the situation. Work on slowing down before coming to a decision. It is good that you are optimistic and have faith in yourself, but stay grounded in the facts and not the theory. You are healthier and happier when you are busy. Boredom caused by a lack of useful or exciting things to do is kryptonite to you. Travel, even if it is only a day trip or an afternoon outing, will do you a great deal of good. You do have a need for freedom and a desire to explore new territories. This applies to all parts of your life, inner and outer. You tend to be happier with friends and loved ones who give you lots of space and love to work and/or adventure with you.

The auras of people with Sagittarius Moon are the most adaptable of the fire Moons. You are particularly good at affecting other people's energy or the energy of a place. Like the other fire Moons, your aura is good at cleansing itself, but it is not automatic and requires your conscious choice. The mutable fire of Sagittarius is changeable and can go from a small ember to a pillar of fire that reaches the sky. It is important that you manage your energy, so it is somewhere between the extremes of almost out and furious inferno. This aura has star power when you light it up, and physical and nonphysical beings will look and listen. Spells and workings that rely on assistance from spirits and deities will be effective.

♑
Moon in Capricorn

Capricorn Moon and Sun enhance organization ability and drive for accomplishment, but also increase your tendency toward negativity and self-doubt. Double the earth means more momentum to get things done no matter what is in your way. You have a strong sense of purpose and enough self-discipline to tackle almost anything. When you stay focused on the best of your traits, you are indefatigable and thrive when you are challenged. Much of your success comes from the planning, plotting, and analysis that a Capricorn Moon loves. The downside to this gift is that you can be too serious and worry too much. Schedule time for recreation or it simply won't happen. You also are prone to being too harsh a critic of your own efforts. Don't wait for others to notice your accomplishments, proclaim them. Cut yourself some slack and you'll improve faster. You pride yourself on your poise and self-control, but if you don't relax enough, you will erupt in a memorable way.

This combination produces a smaller tolerance level for listening to complaints or kvetching or signs of giving up. Make it a practice to strengthen your compassion and patience for others. You'll have fewer unnecessary conflicts when you understand people on their own terms. If you do need something to change, try persuasion first rather than applying coercion. You lose in the long run if you are autocratic. At home, you need a partner who has their own accomplishments and projects so that you can bond over strategizing. Mutual support and reciprocity are essential to happiness in your relationships. You are not generally romantic, but you are affectionate, love deeply, and are truly loyal. Create a home and a family of choice that suits you, not what society tries to enforce. Make the home as an adult that you would have wanted as a child.

A Capricorn Moon, like all the earth element Moons, generates an aura that is magnetic and pulls energy inward. What you draw to yourself tends to stick and solidify, so be wary, especially when doing healing work or cleansings. The magick of a Capricorn Moon is excellent at imposing a pattern or creating a container in a working. Your spells and workings tend to be durable. You also have a gift for protective magick and for banishing negative energies and entities. Spells or workings that deal with prosperity, servitors, attracting resources, and cutting off unwanted connections work well for you.

~~~

Moon in Aquarius

This combination produces a forward-thinking Capricorn with a love of the future. In addition to a powerful intellect, you also have strong intuition that counterbalances your thought process. You tend to examine your own life and the state of the world more than most Capricorns. Your imagination is formidable, and if you can create it in your mind, you can find a way to make it happen in the world. You have an aptitude for finding the steps that transform an idea into a reality.

You are also good at assembling a team to make your dreams happen because you are open and approachable. Aquarius makes you more idealistic and ideological than most Capricorns. People tend to see you as less conventional and more experimental, even when you are trying to look conventional. You are imaginative and a rational thinker who is rarely rash in judgments. You are a good storyteller, and stories often work better than rhetoric to make your point. You are good at inspiring others to do their best. You know how to project confident and calm assurance.

You have a gift for making friends and networking. Make sure you find partners and close friends who can keep up or learn to look back and check on them. For you, candor and precise communications are essential for solid relationships. You do love debating everything. Additionally, please remind yourself that people need to specifically and explicitly hear from you that you care about them. This is especially important to keep in mind when you lose yourself in your projects. Whether it is at home or in the world, you can be a source of stability in chaotic times. As much as you like excitement and new things, you need a home base to be content.

Like all the air Moons, the Aquarius Moon encourages a highly mobile and flexible aura. Without a strong focus, the power of an air subtle body becomes scattered and diffuse. If you have an air Moon, an emphasis should be placed on finding and focusing on your center of energy. Grounding is important, but focusing on your core and center is more important. From that center, you can strengthen and stabilize your power. People with Aquarius Moon are good at shaping and holding a specific thoughtform or energy pattern and transferring it to other people or into objects. Your Capricorn energy allows you to use this Moon to find guidance, inspiration, and spells for group cohesion.

Moon in Pisces

This Moon gives great emotional depth and sensitivity. You need to guard your heart because you feel deeply and notice all the details and flaws of the world. You are equally hurt by thoughtless actions or intentional cruelty to you or others. Thicken your skin and put up some shields, but don't harden your beautiful heart. This combination uses much of its energy to be of help and service to others. Most of your ambitions are connected to gaining status in the world so that you can use that power to make the world better. Occasionally you do need a personal quest, a journey, or perhaps just a regular yoga or meditation session to refresh yourself so you can return to your work. Gazing at the ocean, a river, or any water feature is good for you. Music and the arts are your best medicine. If you don't take care of yourself, you'll withdraw from the tasks that make you feel alive.

You have an abundance of imagination and deep wellsprings of creativity that can be applied in the arts, the sciences, or in business. If you don't have enough opportunity for self-expression or block its flow, it can turn into fretting and brooding. You like to please people, which can lead to saying yes, which will pull you off course in life. When you lose your balance, this combo creates a tendency toward wrongly thinking others do not value you. Your physical health also relies on keeping yourself in equilibrium. In matters of the heart, you are very giving, and when you love someone, you overlook their flaws. You know how to be romantic and affectionate. You'd do better with a partner who is at least as far along in emotional and spiritual development as you are.

With a Pisces Moon, the emphasis should be on learning to feel and control the rhythm of your energetic motion in your aura. Water Moon sign auras are flexible, cohesive, and magnetic, so they tend to ripple and rock like waves. Pisces Moon is the most likely to pick up and hang on to unwanted emotions or energies. Be careful, develop good shielding practices, and make cleansing yourself and your home a regular practice. Pisces Moon people are the best at energizing, comforting, and healing disruptions in other people's auras. This combination is blessed with a gift for healing, soul retrieval, divination, and mediumship.

TAROT
CORRESPONDENCES

♑

You can use the tarot cards in your work as a Capricorn witch for more than divination. They can be used as focal points in meditations and trance to connect with the power of your sign or element or to understand them more fully. They are great on your altar as an anchor for the powers you are calling. You can use the Minor Arcana cards to tap into Jupiter, Mars, or Sun in Capricorn energy even when they are in other signs in the heavens. If you take a picture of a card, shrink the image and print it out; you can fold it up and place it in spell bags or jars as an ingredient.

Capricorn Major Arcana

The Devil

All the Earth Signs

The Ace of Pentacles

Capricorn Minor Arcana

2 of Pentacles	Jupiter in Capricorn
3 of Pentacles	Mars in Capricorn
4 of Pentacles	Sun in Capricorn

• MY MOST CAPRICORN WITCH MOMENT •

Maria Wander

Being a witch involves knowing that we are magic. I know I am magic, and no one can stop my magical ass from being so! I am created in the image of the Goddess, in the image of Mother Nature, made of star stuff—literally everything I am is connected to the world, the universe, and interconnected with everything. This is why magic works.

After high school, I told my parents I was going to be a computer nurse. They told me that career wasn't an actual thing and that I'd have to pay my own way if I wanted to attend college. Saturn can bring achievement and resilience as well as scarcity and privation, so to work my way through college for the necessary science courses, I got a few jobs and did a lot of magic. Ultimately, I won a full scholarship, which covered my bachelor's degree in nursing. A graduation gift from my parents was a book on nursing informatics, a new field in healthcare—computer nursing. I became an emergency room

nurse and a traveling nurse, excellent roles for a Capricorn—
life or death, emergent and always popping. New York City
ER, especially at the full Moons, honed my Capricornian
quick judgment, resilience, and lifesaving resourcefulness.

I went on working at the ER and working on my magic,
and I obtained a second full scholarship toward a master's
degree and a state-of-the-art home computer system fully
stocked with peripherals from the university. Score! That
same year, the seventh year after my graduation as a nurse,
a TV series began shooting episodes in one of the hospi-
tals where I worked. When they mistakenly blew a water
pipe just above the ER, I took charge, organizing patients to
safety. I barked commands to the new hospital director who
walked into the fracas. He'd watched as others stepped away
from the confusion and later he described me as the calm eye
in the middle of a hurricane. The next day I was promoted to
Nurse Administrative Officer, responsible for the entire city
block of the medical center in the evening. Boom!

In hospital, I was able to advance my computer knowledge. On making rounds, I learned that computers liked me
back. I would find staff yelling at their computers and I'd
stop by to push in any peripheral cords that had come loose
while they had been pulling at the keyboard or workstation
to bring the computer back online. Capricorns know that

the solution to the problem is often simple and right in front of us.

Some employees were also grumpy with their coworkers, which is not conducive for good patient care. I listened to and addressed their concerns. To enhance harmony and emotional stability and clear negative stress, I projected energy out from a crystal grid. I set up the grid next to a page torn from a hospital magazine depicting happy clinicians in scrubs working together. When asked what I thought had generated the suddenly increased amity in staff interactions, reducing problematic issues, I indicated how personalized support for the staff was the key.

Have I mentioned that I love astrology? Learning the language of the planets and their cycles is a great joy in my life. I implemented astrology in my magic as soon as I learned that I could. Annually on the Aries new Moon, I schedule a "crafternoon," setting out my witchy intentions to create a vision board. The Aries new Moon is one of the most magical days of the year, the first new Moon of the astrological new year when the Sun crosses on to the Aries Point of 0 degrees Aries. I've done this artsy magic purposefully and intuitively for nearly twenty years. It is amazing to look back at the end of each year and see what is represented on the board that has been realized in my life.

One year, I affixed images of a local Ivy League university and a coven of witches amid astrological symbols. I hadn't planned then for further higher education. I'd stepped back from the British Trad Wicca groups I'd degreed in. I liked the artistry of those images and included them in my annual collation intuitively. This was seven years after I had begun working in the health computing field. Seven is a Saturn number. It identifies the waxing square, a period when the individuation of identity is developed and tested by others and the environment. It is a time when the universe asks us to recommit to our natal Saturnian potential, and so situations arise to nudge us to do just that. I was at the beginning cusp of that Saturn square.

Before year's end, I'd been asked to present one of my evidence-based practice implementations at a prestigious research academy conference. My project was selected as a best practice. A number of medical centers and hospital systems implemented my work as a system change. The associate dean for that Ivy university in my vision board asked me to take part in their new healthcare informatics certification program, attending gratis on a grant. Grant-based Ivy informatics certificate? Boom! The astrology chart for that moment has Saturn on my Midheaven, the highest point, angular and strong. This is a culmination point in career when you are recognized for your achievement and gain respect of colleagues as a leader, or it can be a moment of downfall if you have not been doing the work of your path.

My picture ran in an industry journal as a New York Notable Nurse and one of my witchy friends in healthcare reached out to me to guest at a Wicca study group being run by his tradition, which has a deep basis in magical astrology. I attended a magical astrology workshop their tradition elders were hosting and guested in the study group, which became a coven. I went on to be its first degreed witch and High Priestess. The astrology sign for that new coven? Yes, Capricorn—boom!

The semblance of effortless Capricorn success comes from our persistent, organized outlay of time and effort toward goals. We honor our mentors, elders, ancestors, and age-old knowledge, craftsmanship, value, and quality.

At an autumnal gathering of witches, an elder was wearing a particularly fine hat. It was beautifully fashioned with complex stitches and nubby, earthtone fibers. As I admired it and wondered aloud where such a garment could be acquired, I felt the presence of my goddess patron focusing me in that moment. I was told the hat was an original, hand-knit from handspun.

I felt deeply that I must learn fiber structure, design, hand spinning, knitting—all the tactile textile things. Handmade textiles originated over twenty thousand years ago. Nothing whets the Capricorn appetite more than having control and gaining mastery in an ancient unfolding process, celebrating each transition point of manifestation. I set about to do just that—to hand-process fibers, dye, spin, and knit.

I found a spinning teacher one hundred miles from home for an hour-long bare basics class. I rented a wheel and practiced. I took classes at Rhinebeck Sheep and Wool, obtained tools at Maryland Sheep and Wool, joined a spinning guild, did Master Spinner levels at a Canadian agricultural college, and completed textile/design curricula at the Fashion Institute of New York. Visiting farms, working with the animals, shearing, washing, and processing the fleece or planting, growing, harvesting the flax, breaking, retting, and combing the flax into fiber, dyeing, knitting, and weaving—I did it all in communion with spirit, as a daily practice of creative moving meditation. Throughout I feel a sacred connection to the deities of textiles, who have power over the threads of all creation. Spinning fiber and knitting a garment of handspun is a monumental act of faith. I believe the Goddess brought that hat to my attention because I had been immersed in an urban concrete technological life. I lived and worked in NYC high-rise buildings, operating computers for much of the day and going out nightly to electronic raves. She brought me back to Earth.

Seven years later, my aesthetic came to the notice of a design director who asked me to contribute swatches for a client. Remember that seven is a Saturn number. I was in the tail end of that waxing Saturn square Saturn, the period particularly extended due to retrograde motion of the planet. Planets in astrology, other than the Sun and Moon, retrograde and appear to move backward and forward on their celestial path. Saturn as the slowest of these visible planets takes time to lead up to outcomes. Those outcomes bear the fruit of the quality and type of effort that went into the work.

Over that winter, I fabricated large handmade work. While walking with my Mr. to Lincoln Center in the spring, he gestured at items in a sidewalk shop display window, commenting on their familiarity. I laughed, reminding him that he'd seen those designs in my hands at home. The astrology chart of the moment had Saturn in my tenth house, the most elevated house and natural home of Capricorn, making a golden triangle to my own natal Saturn—a beneficial aspect of earned recognition for our endeavors when we are seen by the world for our skills. My designs had been reworked by Williams Sonoma Home into a multitude of houseware textiles as wall hangings, bedspreads, throw rugs, blankets, pillows, and hassock covers gloriously displayed in window after window on Broadway. Boom!

YOUR RISING SIGN'S INFLUENCE

Ivo Dominguez, Jr.

The rising sign, also known as the ascendant, is the sign that was rising on the eastern horizon at the time and place of your birth. In the birth chart, it is on the left side of the chart on the horizontal line that divides the upper and lower halves of the chart. Your rising sign is also the cusp of your first house. It is often said that the rising sign is the mask that you wear to the world, but it is much more than that. It is also the portal through which you experience the world. The sign of your ascendant colors and filters those experiences. Additionally, when people first meet you, they meet your rising sign. This means that they interact with you based on their perception of that sign rather than your Sun sign. This in turn has an impact on you and how you view yourself. As they get to know you over time, they'll meet you as your Sun sign. Your ascendant is like the colorful clouds that hide the Sun at dawn, and as the Sun continues to rise, it is revealed.

The rising sign will also have an influence on your physical appearance as well as your style of dress. To some degree, your voice, mannerisms, facial expressions, stance, and gait are also swayed by the sign of your ascendant. The building blocks of your public persona come from your rising sign. How you arrange those building blocks is guided by your Sun sign, but your Sun sign must work with what it has been given. For witches, the rising sign shows some of the qualities and foundations for the magickal personality you can construct. The magickal personality is much more than simply shifting into the right headspace, collecting ritual gear, lighting candles, and so on. The magickal persona is a construct that is developed through your magickal and spiritual practices to serve as an interface between different parts of the self. The magickal persona, also known as the magickal personality, can also act as a container or boundary so that the mundane and magickal parts of a person's life can each have its own space. Your rising also gives clues about which magickal techniques will come naturally to you. This chapter describes the twelve possible arrangements of rising signs with a Capricorn

Sun and what each combination produces. There are 144 possible kinds of Capricorn when you take into consideration the Moon signs and rising signs. You may wish to reread the chapter on your Moon sign after reading about your rising sign so you can better understand these influences when they are merged.

Aries Rising

This combination yields one of the strongest potentials for success. Aries Moon provides willpower and Capricorn adds a savvy understanding of the rules of life. This is a forceful combo with high aspirations and tons of energy, but be careful as this can make you overly combative. This rising makes you crave the excitement that change provides. You are more fitness focused and physically active than most Capricorns. However, be mindful that you need rest as well, and inflammation is a warning sign that you've done too much.

Both your Sun and rising are in cardinal signs, so you have a big personality that gets you noticed. When you balance this well, it is charming, and when you don't, you forget to be kind. Learn to give small warnings so that people know when to give you space. You are much more passionate than most Capricorns. You probably need to move more slowly in picking trusted friends and partners. Wait until you are ready before committing to someone. You get more comfortable and adept at making the best of social settings as you age. This comes as you learn to relax, something that is not inherent in your rising and Sun sign.

An Aries rising means that when you reach out to draw in power, fire will answer faster and more intensely. Use your Capricorn earth to control the fire that you call. When working with air or water, use your rising to tune in to air and your Sun to tune in to water. This combination makes it easier for you to raise energy, focus on intentions, and break through obstacles. Charging magickal objects in a lasting way is one of your gifts. The creation of servitors, amulets, and charms is favored as well. This rising also amplifies protective magick for yourself and others.

Taurus Rising

A Taurus rising radiates a quiet powerful strength. Being a double earth sign, you like to know all the details and check your options before taking a step. Once you make up your mind, it is hard to change your opinion. Work on becoming more flexible and adaptable rather than wasting energy on resisting change. You are very resilient and can reach almost any goal you set for yourself. You are more laid back and have a greater need for quiet times and a cozy home than most Capricorns. You are cautious about spending money except when it improves the quality of your life and that of your beloveds. When you do get upset, it is a sight to behold and surprises people.

Your stability and calming presence will endear you to people. It is easier for you to talk about other people's emotions, but you are shy when it comes to expressing yours. Working with people teaches you how to show your heart. People are more important than things, and that is one of your recurring life lessons. You would do well working with plants, with the natural sciences, as a chef, as an entrepreneur, or as anything else that is anchored in the physical world. You do have some artistic or crafting flair and that is where you can release stress.

Taurus rising strengthens your aura and the capacity to maintain a more solid shape to your energy. This gives you stronger shields and allows you to create thoughtforms and spells that are longer lasting. This combination makes it a bit harder to call energy, but once it is started, the flow is strong. You have a powerful gift for financial magick, house blessing or clearing, and rites of passage. This combo also makes it easier to work with nature spirits and plant spirits in particular.

Ⅱ

Gemini Rising

This rising sharpens your communication skills and makes your words compelling. You have a great deal of tact and poise, so the arts of diplomacy are easily mastered. You are more inquisitive about everything and everyone than most Capricorns. You are likely to be a lifelong learner and may shift careers several times. The enthusiasm and adaptability of Gemini strongly assist your Capricorn nature in reaching its goals. To relax, try knitting, painting, carving, playing a musical instrument, juggling, or anything that uses your hands in a skillful way. These sorts of activities greatly reduce stress and improve mental focus.

You come across as openminded and reasonable, so people don't notice how you arrange things to create your security and status. You tend to treat your friends as if they were family and your family as if they were friends. Usually this works, but when it doesn't, quickly adjust how you see and treat the person who doesn't like this arrangement. Your emotional connection to people usually only comes with two settings, on or off. Try to add a few more settings or at the least make sure everyone knows how you function so they don't conclude that you don't care.

This combination makes you skilled at writing spells and rituals that make good use of whatever resources you have at hand. This rising helps your energy and aura stretch farther and to adapt to whatever it touches. You would do well to develop your psychic skills as well as practices such as telepathy, empathy, and energy healing. You can pick up too much information and that can be overwhelming, so training is essential. Learn to close and control your awareness of other people's thoughts and feelings. You may have a gift for interpreting dreams and the words that come from oracles and seers. This combination often has a knack for knowing how best to use music, chanting, and drumming in magick.

Cancer Rising

You tend to be more emotional and more reserved than most others of your sign. You show caring through material gestures such as food, gifts, the gift or your time, and the opening of your heart. You are an excellent listener and rarely give advice, but when you do, it is gentle and precise. You have a limited amount of time before you are done with being around people. Plan when and how you will use your supply of *people* energy. Recharging at home is the best course for self-care. You want to go with your intuition much of the time, but that is not a good idea. Choose to use your intellect so you are not ruled by your emotions. An even mix of head and heart will steer you right.

You have a love of history, anthropology, folklore, genealogy, museums, and such. This can bring you great joy and activities that you treasure your whole life. These interests may shape your career choices. You need to find work that feeds your soul as well as your bank account. You get things done so smoothly that your efforts aren't always noticed. In matters of love, you make sure you find someone who is as sentimental as you are. The health of your gut is strongly affected by your emotional state; use it as an indicator to attend to your distress.

Cancer grants the power to use your emotions, or the emotional energy of others, to power your witchcraft. Though you can draw on a wide range of energies to fuel your magick, raising power through emotion is the simplest. You may also have a calling for dreamwork, past-life recall, or dowsing. Moon magick for practical workings for abundance or healing of the heart comes easily for you. Your spells or workings for blessing yourself or other people are particularly effective.

Leo Rising

This rising brings a sunnier and more optimistic perspective than is common for Capricorns. Leo self-confidence and poise amplify and support your drive for achievement. You have more style and sparkle than most Capricorns. This combination makes you a natural at leading, inspiring, and managing people. You have a good sense of humor that helps you smooth over the troubles that come with roles of authority. You may be drawn to work in finance, healthcare, or education. Public service is also a possible career path. Whatever you do must match your sense of honor and dignity.

Although you are cordial and appear to have many friends, your actual circle is small. This is because you are so good at looking warm and welcoming. You prefer quality over quantity in most things in life. You are loyal and tend to forgive offenses swiftly, though you never forget them. You are generous with those in your inner circle. Be as kind to yourself as you are to others. In matters of love and friendship, you are a bit complicated to understand. Your Sun and rising are like a kaleidoscope of fire and ice. You take your time revealing yourself. Be patient as those close to you get to see and understand your inner self. Your partners will adore you once you come into focus.

Leo rising means that when you reach out to draw in power, fire will answer easily. Lean into your Capricorn earth to control fire. Earth answers your call through the power of your Sun, and fire through your rising sign. Your aura and energy are brighter and steadier than most people's, so you attract the attention of spirits, deities, and so on. Whether or not showing up so clearly in the other worlds is a gift or a challenge is up to you. Your Sun and rising give you a gift for leading and writing rituals.

Virgo Rising

Capricorn's drive and Virgo's eye for details gives you what it takes to excel. You are a keen observer of the world who notices the pertinent details. You have a strong intellect, so you scan, cram, and sort information with speed and skill. It does make you a bit crazy when you must engage in group efforts when you are sure you'd be better off doing it all yourself. The downside to this mix is that you find it harder to show your true emotions. You default to a serious and reserved demeanor when you are in public. You are amazing, but you must let people see other facets of your nature. When stressed, you may become overly suspicious. Take it as a sign you need a break.

To have successful close relationships, you need people who are comfortable with the amount of space and time you need. Ideally, they also have many projects of their own to keep them busy. You also do better with people who also have a love of structure. In your personal life and work life, refrain from focusing on flaws and errors. You can get caught up in unproductive cycles of thoughts and feelings. It is also important to know that sometimes you do have to bend or break the rules for better outcomes.

Virgo rising with a Capricorn Sun makes it easier to work with goddesses and gods who are connected to the element of earth, plant life, agriculture, academic pursuits, and commerce. You have a gift for creating connections between different kinds of magick. Magickal research, divination, oracular work, and cord cutting (separation magick) are favored by this combination. Be careful when you entwine your energy with someone else because you can pick up and retain their patterns and issues. Always cleanse your energy after doing solo or collective work.

♎

Libra Rising

Your Capricorn ambitions are expressed with creativity and artistry through this rising. You know how to sound, what to wear, and how to pull off all the little nonverbal cues of a culture, scene, or in-group. It does cost you energy to do this, but it is one of your superpowers. Your warmth can melt away most icy obstacles. You are an excellent negotiator, dealmaker, and arbiter. Under that Libra façade, you have the hard determination of a Capricorn. You say yes to more work too often, so it would be valuable to learn more about time management methods.

Your weakness is that you are much more sensitive and shyer than you appear on the surface. It is not long until you need some alone time to recharge.

Learning to take risks in small, measured steps to build courage will improve all parts of your life. When you are overwhelmed, you tend to get stuck and lock up. It is important that you plan for obstacles and manage your emotional reserves as well. If something can't get past something, move on without it and try again later. The more your day-to-day life matches your aesthetics, the more vitality you will have. Artistic activities that make use of your Capricorn detail focus are enlivening for you. Your body responds quickly to your thoughts and feelings, so be kind to it.

Libra rising with a Capricorn Sun wants to express its magick through the creation of things. You may carve and dress candles, create sumptuous altars, write beautiful invocations, or create amazing ritual wear. You also know how to bring together people who use different types of magick and arrange smooth collaborations. You are good at spell work for making peace, laying spirits to rest, attracting familiars, and self-love. Try your hand at crystal magick, herbalism, charms, and house blessings as they would suit your talents.

Scorpio Rising

This combination is intense and likes to live life on the edge. You live in the moment, but you want to know all the details and backstory that lead to each moment. Everything you do is part of your plan to get what you want. If you feel blocked from reaching your goals, this combination can lead you to be seen as domineering or insensitive. Compromise does not come easily to you, but sarcasm does. It is important to control your passionate nature as it can get the better of you. When you give your heart to love, friendship, or a purpose, you do it fully and with great vigor. You can be a stalwart ally and defender, especially when the odds are not in your favor.

You are imaginative and intuitive and might do well as a lawyer, a planner, a therapist, a writer, and, of course, a witch. You are cunning and perhaps too wary of other people's motives. Capricorn and Scorpio have different approaches to life, which creates an internal tension between the rational and the emotional. Turn these tensions into shades of gray or, better yet, a full rainbow to access your power. Look to the rest of your chart, life experience, and input from friends to find the middle ground.

Scorpio rising makes your energy capable of cutting through most energetic barriers. You can dissolve illusion or bring down wards or shields and see through to the truth. You may have an aptitude for breaking curses and lifting oppressive spiritual atmospheres. Your magick has the power of deep change, revelation, and regeneration. You have a knack for spells related to transformation, finding hidden or lost things, and revealing past lives. It is important that you do regular cleansing work for yourself. You are likely to end up doing messy work, and you do not have a nonstick aura.

Sagittarius Rising

This rising's enthusiasm and vision combined with your Sun's need to organize and work can make you great at whatever you choose to do. With Sagittarius's ruling planet of Jupiter, you are more cheerful than other Capricorns. The relentless Sagittarius energy combines well with practical Capricorn. This combination gives you a wide scope of vision and interests, but unless you keep centered, these can also lead to excess and spreading yourself too thin. That said, you tend to always bounce back and are successful. You are responsible and conscientious in work matters; remember to do the same for friends and loved ones.

You love to travel and are equally interested in cultures, landscapes, and meeting new people. You have an unquenchable thirst to learn about just about everything. Thankfully you have an abundance of mental energy that is a passion of the mind. You are very idealistic and bound to your personal code of honor. It is likely that you can turn off your emotions for the sake of clarity and efficiency. This is useful, but it may cause you to worry that you are coldhearted. This is not true unless you choose to always throttle back your feelings. You are very selective about who you allow into your inner circle.

Your magick is stronger when you are standing outside on the ground. Your rising sign's fire can become a pillar of flame in your hearth. You have a gift for helping others open their spiritual talents and you act as a catalyst to empower group rituals. You have a talent for workings and spells that call forth creativity, wisdom, and freedom. Devotional work with altars, icons, or statues helps you. If you do astral travel or soul journeying, be sure all of you is back and in its proper place within you.

Capricorn Rising

Double Capricorn makes you the epitome of tenacity and thoroughness. This double earth combination encourages you to be practical, precise, and exacting. You are serious and stately and, if you are not careful, somber. You do work harder and play less than most. However, on those rare occasions when you let loose, you are a party animal. Your challenge is to make sure that you keep a good balance in your life. It is easy for you to get so enthralled with your tasks that you neglect spending quality time with people who care about you. You are independent and can go long stretches without much human contact, but even camels need to drink water.

You are drawn to large-scale or long-term projects, and you are good at guiding and supporting people in these endeavors. You are good at keeping up to date with the changes in the world because you know that is needed to remain effective. You tend to be a stabilizing influence in the lives of those you interact with. In matters of love or close friendship, do not let worry over loss prevent you from sharing yourself with others. You need people to share your successes. Your joints and your stomach may be sensitive, so be kind to them.

Capricorn rising creates an aura and energy field that is slow to come up to speed but has amazing momentum once fully activated. Make it your habit to do some sort of energy work or meditative warmup or breath work before engaging in witchcraft. Try working with crystals, stones, and geographic features like mountains as your magick blends well with them. Working with time itself and timing helps your magick. You are especially good at warding and spells to make long-term changes. You may have a commanding voice that the spirits hear.

Aquarius Rising

There is somewhat of a dichotomy between a rising that loves thought and abstractions and a Capricorn Sun that wants to keep things practical and grounded. Rather than being a problem, this dynamic tension gives you more energy to pursue your goals and tend to your duties. There is also a great deal of trust in your self-worth. You are more innovative and experimental than most others of your sign. You approach most things in life with great verve and precision. You see the world very differently than most and this gives you a quirky sense of humor. You also get joy from finding new ways to circumvent the rules of the game of life.

This combination makes for original thinking and moments of genius. You take a great interest in matters that affect the world and have a reforming spirit. Boredom will damage your health more than stress, so stay active. This combination can appear cool because of your capacity for objective detachment. However, when your role is providing support or service for someone, you are accommodating and conscientious. All matters of your heart begin with friendship and cooperation that then lead to feelings. When you do commit to friendship or love, you are devoted and steady in your connection and affection.

Aquarius rising helps you consciously change the shape and density of your aura. This makes you a generalist who can adapt to many styles and forms of magick. Witchcraft focused on increasing intuition, analysis of problems, and release from blockages is supported by this combination. Visualization can play an important role in your magick and meditations. If you aren't particularly good at visualization, focus the spoken word to tune in to your power. You have a gift for working with thought-forms and spirits that give information and seeing the big picture.

Pisces Rising

You come across as sympathetic, kind, and a touch otherworldly. Your Pisces-inspired psychic perceptions connect you with other people's feelings and thoughts. Lean into your Capricorn Sun to provide you with the structure to use these gifts well. Whether by logic or intuition, you find the simplest and most effective solutions to problems for other people or situations. If you are trying to solve your own problems, slow down and double-check all the details. You are guided and often protected, but don't make your spirit helpers work too hard. You can excel in a wide range of fields, but you are not very mainstream, so you have to create your own career path.

You are affectionate and want romance with all the bells and whistles. When you are in love, you open completely and are quite vulnerable. Unfortunately, you tend to cling to your memories of past experiences, which can affect your current relationships. Work on letting things go and take your time in opening up to your partners. You have a deep need for connection that must push through some bashfulness. Regular spiritual work helps keep you on an even keel. Animals, music, and the arts in general are among the best medicines for your body, mind, and spirit.

Pisces rising connects your Capricorn Sun with the other planes of reality. Your power, as a witch, flows when you do magick to open the gates to the other worlds. You have a special gift for creating sacred space, blessing places, and working with ley lines. You can do astral travel, hedge riding, and soul travel in all its forms with some training and practice. You can help others find their psychic gifts. You may have an aptitude for the healing arts, especially in modes that rely on herbalism, energy work, or guided visualization.

A DISH FIT FOR A CAPRICORN: BOUNTIFUL BLESSINGS BOURGUIGNON

Dawn Aurora Hunt

* * *

You are impressive, Capricorn. Your organizational skills are just what you need to create one of the most celebrated dishes of all time. This French stew, made with tender cuts of brisket and copious amounts of red wine, is a meal for only the discerning diner and requires attention to detail, with many steps to get the desired dish. Though this recipe has been simplified and is much easier than Julia Child's version, it is still bound to impress. What makes this dish so delectable has always been the rich wine gravy. Magically, beef has long been associated with prosperity and wealth, and wine holds energy of bounty, gratitude, and abundance.

Note: If your diet precludes you from eating animal protein, you may try this recipe with a meatless option, such as Gardein beefless tips or a comparable product. You will also want to substitute the bacon with a meatless version and use vegetable broth instead of beef broth. If made with real meat, this recipe is gluten-free.

Ingredients:

+ 3 pounds beef brisket cut into chunks
+ Salt to taste
+ 6 slices bacon, chopped
+ Olive oil
+ 1 large carrot, peeled and chopped
+ 1 large celery rib, chopped
+ 1 large yellow onion, chopped
+ 6 cloves garlic, minced
+ Pepper to taste
+ 3 cups red wine (Burgundy, Merlot, or Pinot Noir)
+ 2 tablespoons cornstarch
+ 2½ cups beef broth
+ 3 tablespoons tomato paste
+ 2 teaspoons Worcestershire sauce
+ 3 bay leaves
+ 1 tablespoon fresh thyme, chopped
+ 1 tablespoon fresh rosemary, chopped
+ 1 tablespoon fresh parsley, chopped
+ 1 pound fresh mushrooms, sliced
+ 2 tablespoons butter
+ Mashed potatoes and/or French bread (optional)

Directions:

Bring beef to room temperature. Pat the beef dry with a paper towel, season with a pinch of salt, and set aside. In a large skillet on medium heat, sauté bacon until brown and crisp. Remove the bacon from the pan and set aside, leaving the bacon fat in the frying pan. Add olive oil to the bacon fat and heat for just one minute so that all the fats are the same temperature before cooking the beef. Brown the beef, searing each piece on all sides until browned. Transfer cooked beef and cooked bacon to a five-quart slow cooker. In the remaining oil/bacon fat in the skillet, sauté the carrots, celery, onion, and four cloves of garlic just until sizzling. Once sizzling, remove the vegetables to the slow cooker as well. Season with salt and pepper and toss all the ingredients together until combined.

In the same skillet as you prepared the vegetables and meats, pour the red wine and simmer on medium heat for about five minutes. Whisk in the cornstarch until no lumps are seen. Continue to simmer, thickening slightly another five minutes. Add the wine to the slow cooker. Add the broth, tomato paste, Worcestershire, fresh herbs, and salt and pepper to taste. Cook in the slow cooker on high heat for five hours or low heat for eight to ten hours, until beef is falling apart when touched with a fork.

Five to ten minutes before serving, cook the mushrooms. In a medium skillet, heat the butter and two cloves of garlic until fragrant. Add the mushrooms to the garlic butter and cook about five minutes while stirring so they don't stick. When they have slightly wilted, add the mushrooms to the stew and gently fold until they are fully combined. Serve the Bourguignon over mashed potatoes or with French bread for dipping.

RECHARGING AND SELF-CARE

Maria Wander

Capricorn self-care is nature based and grounded in connection with the natural world. We are spirit come to Earth, installed in wonderful physical forms. Caring well for our amazing vehicles does take effort. The best way to recharge is to immerse restfully with quality downtime. Capricorns know the first step to doing anything successfully is to actually take a first step. A good way to start is by making lists, and from there, making plans. The act of expressing and recording our ideas, thoughts, and opinions into the manifest world will then make space in our beautiful brain for new thoughts and for good rest. There are no rules for this, only a caution—this practice is not a focus on negative thoughts or emotions; we are not digging a mental hole to drop into and bury ourselves. This practice is an opportunity to jot down what is bothering us but also what lifts us up. Journaling in detail to relive upsetting events is not part of this practice.

Capricorn Mountaintop Mind Dump

Get through thoughts that crowd the brain and stress the rest of the body by getting them out and down on paper. Organizing in this way increases self-awareness and boosts focus by freeing up our internal bandwidth. Have a notebook and get ready to write. Start off with a brief calming meditation by breathing deep, slow, and easy. Then in your mind's eye, envision climbing like a goat up the face of a mountain until you find a cozy ledge to rest and watch the Sun starting to make its descent in the sky. We can't rest well unless we have some sense of accomplishment first. Now let your words and ideas flow from you without judgment or concerns about spelling or proper phrasing.

+ What do I choose to accomplish the following day, week, month.
+ What relationships do I want to make more time for and how will I do that.
+ What concerns are weighing on me.
+ What should I note down to recall what I've been putting off.
+ What realizations did I have today, any images or symbols of note to consider.
+ What am I worried about.
+ What makes me happy today.
+ What thoughts are holding me back.

+ What did I achieve today.
+ What were the highs and lows for the day, the week, the month.

Give negative self-talk, fears, and doubts a break by leaving off words like *need to* or *have to* that form unnecessary pressure or the *should have, could have, would haves* that generate apprehension and regret for missed opportunities. Using this practice as a restful avenue to have compassion for ourselves connects us to our power and acknowledges what is weighing on us, where we are overextending, and what can lift us out of our struggles. Cataloging what we choose and want to do places the agency where it should be, positioned beneficially with ourselves.

Capricorns stoke our engines of energy by fueling all our incessant preparations and developments with Saturnian staying power. With this long-term planning, we often don't take enough care of ourselves in the short term. We owe it to ourselves to schedule in quality self-care by maximizing this as the first thing we do daily. It may sound counterintuitive since, upon awakening, we've hopefully just slept the night away to meet the day well rested. Maybe we have, maybe we haven't; in either case, using the first moments of the day to connect with ourselves is one of the most enriching ways to create a restorative practice as a priority. Take this time out to journal for five to ten minutes, listen to a short guided meditation track that nourishes hope and resilience, or go for a brief walk out in nature.

Renew with *Re-*

Unlike the primary celestial lights of the Sun and Moon, the remaining planets have a retrograde cycle when they take their own steps back to recharge, appearing to move in reverse up in the sky. Humans aren't the only ones who need a break now and then! Retrograde periods recall us to rest and to renew, regenerate, refresh, reflect, retreat, reclaim, review, revise, refocus, release, revive, rethink, reevaluate, revisit, reconsider, reconnect, redo, reassess, reenvision, and retry. These are all good *re* word reminders that give us space and time to gather our strength and look to stocking our energy reserves. We can't make those planned potions if our cauldron is running on fumes. Explore each of these *re* terms in relation to how you use your resources by applying them in the mountaintop mind dump practice at the change of the season. This timing routine will ritualize looking back at interests and involvements pursued that have filled our lives for that time. We are so often focused on the future; the act of being present and then looking back creates a restful frame that is not projecting us forward into what needs doing. That sense of connection to ourselves and where we've been does help relax us in the path we've chosen.

Consistent routine works for amped-up adults as much as it does for little ones, especially a bedtime routine. Often, we have busy lives and a lot of considerations to juggle. These take up parking space in our system, engines firing, emitting fretful fumes that preclude restful sleep. Wind down your day well so that you sleep soundly.

Goodnight Self-Care

A clean sweep makes for good sleep. Take your besom to each room corner and sweep toward the open door, envisioning any stagnant or unrestful energy departing. Keep bedsheets fresh by changing them at least once a week. Take a warm bath or shower and consciously remove the "not you" with bodywash containing sea salt or pink Himalayan salt or make your own bath salts with ½ cup Epsom salt; ½ cup sea, pink Himalayan, or kosher salt; and five drops each lavender and valerian essential oils. Pour into the bath and soak for twenty minutes. Afterward get in bed with your journal; write the date and something you are grateful for. Savor the feeling that this brings to you. Sleep with an eye mask and earplugs to keep the spirit light orbs and night trolls at bay. Before nodding off, send out a call to have positive help on the astral plane, bringing clarity and guidance for nagging issues that plague your mind.

Another restful ritual uses the Big Bad Wolf snooze spots. Massage these body points after getting in bed. First take slow, deep breaths, relaxing your eyes, using light pressure for one to two minutes at the first two locations. On the last spot, use firm pressure for about three minutes. One—the better to see you with—is at the center of the brows just above the nose; press here with two fingers. Two—the better to hear you with—is located by positioning your thumbs behind your earlobes, then moving them back toward your neck to the soft indentation just past the bony prominence behind your ear. Position left thumb behind left ear and right thumb behind right ear, elbows out, opening your chest. Three—the better to feet you with—is at the top of the foot in the indentation where big toe connects with the next toe.

There is no bad time for ritual and self-care. If you end the day well, you will be in better condition to start the day well. A good way to start the day is to awaken with ritual. Make ritual habitual. Put the *yes* in *yesterday*; I did that and tomorrow I will do it again. Make that your mantra. When it is time to get up, consciously awaken with a sense of joy and purpose.

Good Day Self-Care
Upon awakening from sleep, do a quick and gentle stretch. See in your mind's eye the first glow of the Sun nearing the horizon. Take a slow deep inhale of the solar energy, as if

each increment of inhalation brings sunup higher, the dawn light growing and growing until the Sun has fully risen. Release that breath slowly. Give yourself a soft hug with chin tucked to chest as if you were holding an egg there. Round your spine outward, pulling your navel inward as you give yourself a squeeze. Relax your chin and slowly open up your chest, puffing it out and extending forward with your heart. Pull arms back and slightly arch your spine; yawn, stretch, and relax and say internally or aloud,

> *Thank you, Ancestors, Lord, and Lady, for this day.*
> *Thank you, Spirit, Guides, and Mother Earth, for*
> *   helping in every way.*

Think of someone you're thankful for and send them good wishes. Next, think on who is challenging your last nerve and send them good wishes. Feel the Sun shining upon you and send yourself good wishes.

Green Self-Care

Now that you have cleared your mind, rested well, and arisen with pleasure and intention, connect with the earth. Touch earth regularly by gardening and working with herbs. Grow herbs in a witch's garden outdoors or with indoor containers. Start with hardy perennials like yarrow, lemon balm, and rosemary. Border wild growers that extend like mint or mugwort.

Make magical items with herbs; it's delightfully witchy. I gather stalks from my garden, soak them, and braid them together and fasten the edges with ribbon or yarn. Sometimes I braid ribbon in. I use these to decorate altars and as wands for spells, some of which I burn as an offering at the end of a working.

Wreath crowns can also be made from herbs in the same manner by connecting the herbal stems into a circle. For a sturdier crown, use floral tape and floral wire. Create a circle with the wire a little larger than the crown of your head. Wrap the circle all the way around using the floral tape. Secure the fresh herbs in small bunches and wrap wire from the middle of the stalk down to the base of the bunch. Leave a tail of wire at the end of the bunch to attach the bunch to the crown. Tuck the end of the tail in under a length of the wire so it does not poke out. Once attached, wrap floral tape around the base of the bunch to cover the wire. Continue with additional bunches of herbs, moving each bunch back around the wire of the crown until you achieve a pleasing balance.

Use herbs for herbal wands and crowns. Infuse with special intention for an additional layer of magic coupled with the natural magic of the plant spirit. Lavender helps concentration, calms nerves, and focuses the mind. Chamomile for protection against negativity, positive energy, confidence, attracting luck, and breaking hexes. Basil for financial abundance, courage, and to enhance business. Sage for healing, wisdom, protection, and purification. Tulsi for awareness, mental clarity, and opening mind and heart to the divine. I often wear a Tulsi crown when writing creatively. Make your own tea blends and drink with consciousness and purpose. Rosemary inspires self-acceptance and self-love, strengthens will, aids memory and intuition, and can shift slump into motivation. Try this with two sprigs of fresh rosemary in boiling water steeped for five minutes with a squeeze of lemon juice and some honey.

The Calming Power of Clarity

Sharon Knight

Lack of clarity can be a great source of anxiety for us Cappies. Capricorns are typically known for "taking care of business," and when our clarity becomes muddied, we lose our "make it happen" mojo. We don't see what move to make next, just a jumble of thoughts, worries, and things that need doing, and we feel overwhelmed. When I find myself trapped in feelings of anxiety and overwhelm, it is often because I am not seeing the situation laid out before me in an organized fashion.

To regain this much desired clarity, I'll share a tarot-based self-care practice that has helped me many times.

You will need:
+ A deck of tarot cards
+ Colored pens, pencils, or markers
+ 3–8 pieces of paper

Instructions:
I like to start with a ritual bath and candles. This gets the gunk of the day off and helps get us focused and present to the working at hand.

Once appropriately refreshed and focused, we'll sit at our altar with a tarot deck, colored pens, and paper, and contemplate the situation from various angles. Group key elements that you are seeking clarity on into words or phrases and write these things on a piece of paper. Then, shuffle your deck, contemplating each word or phrase, and draw a card for each, faceup. This is not a divination where we draw the cards unseen, but an act of magic where we draw cards intentionally, choosing at will the ones that best represent each aspect of our situation.

I recommend drawing no less than two, for simple either/or situations, and no more than seven. More than seven can lead us back into the overwhelm we are seeking refuge from!

Once you have your cards drawn, take an additional piece of paper for each card. Write out what each card gives you and what it requires of you. Place it beneath its corresponding card. Writing it out like this gets our jumbled thoughts out of us, where we can view them more objectively. I like to make my lists as artful as possible, using my best handwriting, colored pens, and decorative squiggles. I find the creative flow involved in making art enhances magic and thus deepens my intuition.

Here is an example: I want to do *all the things, all the time*. And I just can't. So, I am often looking for clarity regarding which projects to prioritize and which to put on hold. Recently I wrote down five separate projects that were vying for my attention, all of which require a good bit of time and commitment. I focused on one project at a time and chose one tarot card that captured the essence of that project. Then I wrote lists for each—first the gifts that project gives me, then what it requires of me, until I had all five projects represented. I made a point to make each list artful, and the variance in my handwriting from list to list definitely prompted some insight. Before I was finished, I had already identified the two that were dearest to my heart. They were the most fun, and also the ones most likely to bring success at this time. Clarity achieved through tarot, lists, and art!

DON'T BLAME IT ON YOUR SUN SIGN

Maria Wander

The Capricorn witch knows all about limitations from boundary-enforcing Saturn, the visible planet farthest from the warmth and light of Sun and Moon. Instead of playing the blame game, avoid getting mired in darkness that is part and parcel of being a Capricorn. For every lower vibration of expression, there is a correspondingly higher one of mastery and wisdom.

Getting Past Perfectionism

Our perfectionism can be traced to Cronus, King of Titans and primordial God of Time who was the OG Capricorn. He and his wife, Rhea, Goddess of Earth, birthed a generation of Olympians whom Cronus promptly swallowed after their birth. Cronus's own father had blocked his progeny's deliveries as well—like his son, discontentedly insecure about the results of his procreative quality. Rhea concealed their son Jove, who could oversee the aspects of life with the power of sky and lightning. Jove vanquished Cronus who disgorged the Olympians. This myth narrates the seeding behind some blameworthy Capricorn behaviors. If you recognize retentiveness, procrastination, or hesitance within yourself, know that the first step to change and expel internal blocks is through awareness, which can illuminate like a lightning bolt.

Perfection is not reality. Good enough is pretty good. But not for the Capricorn witch who hones skills, painstakingly planning and practicing to arrive at desired excellence. No Capricorn likes looking back knowing that they could have nailed it if they had worked harder to be better. Capricorns compete with themselves, and if we are off our game, we delay and postpone to create a situation of requirement that forces us to burst from our inaction.

What blocks our initiative is giving in to the anxiety of thinking we can always improve. We freeze into inactive dread, apprehensive of not hitting that mark. When this happens, recharge yourself with the powers of Rhea. Lie down on the ground. Tuck your shoulder blades with your chest slightly out to support your back. Separate legs with arms alongside your body, slightly separate from torso. Loosen jaw, face, body, and mind. Feel the weight of yourself on the ground for five to ten minutes. The Earth is our most basic support. Take time for conscious connection and let go.

When we get down on ourselves and our imperfections, it also helps us meditate on Saturn as a fertility deity who ruled over the physical earth and the prosperity of the soil. His scythe is a fitting sigil to cut through stasis. To get into flow and past inertia, focus on the outcome of harvest. Picture a farmer scything fields of wheat: back straight, knees bent, feet firmly planted on the ground, torso twisting to pull the scythe back and then forward in effortful strokes, then advancing to the next section. The steps of how to deal with any of our concerns is there. Use tools and our edge. Ground. Connect with the earth in steady rhythm with our work, one step at a time.

Elemental Awareness

Counteracting inflexibility is the work of a lifetime for Capricorn. Concerned with doing the right thing, we freeze in hardline dualistic thinking of the right and wrong way. In striving toward achievement, we can overvalue structure and order. This compounds our natural stolid earthy orientation to inflexibility, keeping a stiff upper lip, and maintaining our composure during times of trouble to avoid the appearance of weakness or revealing the state of our emotions. We fear our vulnerability and build emotional walls that hold back exposing perceived weakness. This creates a somatic tension and emotional rigidity, a character armoring contraction that creates blocks. This can have real physical manifestations of atrophy, brittle dryness, and restricted movement. We can disdain all but high mastery and are unlikely to open up about our struggles. This is why you will see Capricorns emotionally distancing and working on projects or practicing solo. What aids the Capricorn witch is to shift from the rigid past that cannot be changed to skill in elemental navigation.

Elemental awareness practices can release and detoxify fearful emotions held in our mind and body. Aligning the self with the sacred in the elements is the path to engaging and activating our physical and subtle bodies to unlock from our predisposition for fear-based inflexibility. We need to feel our emotions and face them to put our experiences in perspective. Becoming an external observer to our internal processes reduces out-of-proportion fears. We can benefit from Aries and Libra, the signs that square off from Capricorn, and from Cancer, our emotionally intelligent, compassionate teacher that mirrors Capricorn. Squares are astrological aspects of action. Oppositions are the Saturnian aspect of dynamic tensions and otherness. From these signs, Capricorn learns we are never truly without choice. Aries says *just do it*. Libra says *balance all options*. Cancer says *let your emotions guide you*.

Engaging in what brings joy and connecting with the deep guiding principles inherent in us and our Daimon, the guardian spirit of our divine spark, optimizes the release of fear and enhances resilience. This Daimon actualization with earth, air, fire, and water can be accomplished adroitly with deliberate, regular practice. Use a Saturnian slow, methodical pace to optimize your awareness in the present moment. You will need a glass of water nearby prior to beginning.

Start by thinking of something you are grateful for. Envision this completely so that you can hear, smell, taste, or feel the sensations of your experience. Give thanks to your mind that never stops sending you thought and information; for your senses, which illuminate your world with sensations; to your bones, skin, and muscles for giving your body structure; to the rest of your body for the purpose and pleasure it provides; for your immediate location, where you are, the clothes you wear, the food you've consumed; for your external environment, all hands seen and unseen who are part of your life and support you; for the world itself, for nature, for gravity, for the universe and your place in it. Feel the good that surrounds you.

Next, inhale deeply and tighten the pelvic floor muscles in one Kegel, exhaling and releasing an energetic cord from the base of the spine into the core of the Earth. Inhale again and bring up energy from the Earth with the cord as it returns to the base of the spine. Then have a glass of water. As you drink slowly, ask to connect deeply with your Daimon to embody, support and guide your authenticity, healing, and fulfillment of your soul purpose.

Break any internal blocks with the breath of fire and air. Inhale slowly and deeply to fill your lungs, feeling your stomach rise. Locate any tension in your body. Exhale forcefully through your teeth without clamping them or tightening the jaw, allowing the expressed breath to hiss out as if you are a fire-breathing dragon. Envision the air exchange shifting the stasis and releasing blockages so that they become smaller and smaller particulates that you blow out and away.

Tithing

Admittedly, Capricorn is very money conscious, aware of lack and mindful of our finances. We can be Scrooge-like and Grinchy, stingy, miserly, mean, and acquisitively greedy at the same time. Our ruling planet, Saturn, conserves and restricts, bringing hardship and leaving us always wanting more because of a sense of being without or not having enough. Our practical nature makes us blunt and brusque, sharp-tongued, and we can come across as cold, negative, or pessimistic because our ability to discern can easily shift to dissatisfaction and criticism. The remedy to any disorder is its opposite, and fortunately Capricorn's strong sense of responsibility and discipline can support a more mature reaction to restriction. The feelings of lack that many Capricorns may have experienced early in life can become the basis of generosity since we understand well what it is to go without. Understanding what holds true value and learning to appreciate the simple things in life that cannot be purchased or have a price put on them is the key to flipping pessimism into optimism. For every negative thought or setback, review the past through a lens of lessons learned and experience obtained. Rather than being mean in self-talk and treating ourselves with more criticism than we ever would heap onto another person, we can reframe by using the same language and advice we would want shared with us.

To truly release a sense of lack and meanness, tithe to Saturn by donating your time and efforts. Do something to make your world better and do it regularly. Start small and personally. Perhaps make a vow to honor your earthly container and make your body healthier as a sacred discipline, e.g., *I will walk fifteen to twenty minutes or one mile most every day*, or select some scholarship challenge to master. In the struggle comes true learning. Donate your skills to a charity or organization in voluntary charitable service. Honor and help your elders. Educate and teach those who need what knowledge you can provide. In such sacrifice, we honor the archetype of Saturn and remedy malefic influences. The more challenging it is to learn something and the more you work to discover what needs to be done, the better you become at doing that thing. The critic that mocks you, what strikes at your confidence, the doubts that plague you—these are the hauntings of Saturn that are actually a gift. Yes, really! The etymology of the word *gift* comes from *giefu*, which means "natural talent given or ability miraculously conferred." This is the inspiration that, combined with perspiration, results in our genius.

Power days to pay back or pay forward are the days of the Sun's transmigration from one sign into another, specifically the six hours before and after the Sun has changed signs. If you have pending bills, use these power periods to send a payment, even a small one. These are also very auspicious times to meditate, contemplate, send out prayers, journal, and do self-exploration. These are special moments that are hinges of change, a time of shift when doing something new is not ideal. Instead, these periods are for looking back at the past month and reflecting on your challenges, choices, and lessons learned.

We cannot control the fate of our birth date and our assignment as Capricorns, but we can control our experiences of this placement. Reframe challenging situations using the tools in this chapter to provide you with options. Don't let the negative self-talk and doubts prey on your mind. Find another way of looking at the situation and provide yourself with an alternate solution. The Capricorn witch knows that magic is about transformation, progression, and self-acceptance of our power and divinity, our fears and anxieties, the brighter and darker aspects of our nature.

POSTCARD FROM A CAPRICORN WITCH

Aeptha

This story is a day in a Capricorn practitioner's life and Saturn's influence. Ceremonial lodge day begins with a familiar cadence. Rising at the same time each morning aligns with the Sun and the start of the new day. Carefully ritual attire is chosen; the robes hold memories collected from hundreds of ceremonies over thirty-five years. The talisman has remained the same through multiple initiations and is placed around my neck. I feel the frequency of my tradition flowing through me like a river.

Dressed in ritual garb, I stand with the other Lodge members. The outer appearance is one of stillness; inside is intense concentration. The beat of the drum combines with the sound of moving feet as we process into the temple space. Included in my responsibilities after decades of training is the oversight of the ritual. Ritual is a vehicle for the patterning of consciousness, and if done correctly, calculable results are obtained. The opening creates a structured container that supports the work and intent of the ritual. As the adepts perform the opening, I observe on the inner levels the subtle weaving of a complex layering.

I was taught by my initiator that if the procession and opening of the ritual are done correctly, a firm foundation is established. It is from here that you can let human consciousness change or transcend its rhythm. The drummer starts a beat, and a chant begins. Motion fills my body, and there is a gathering up of power and the focus of will. As the ecstatic energy expands, the condition of my consciousness changes, and there is an apprehension of a deeper state of reality. There are protocols and signs; when and if they are met, I open to the influx of a different consciousness as my conscious mind becomes passive. Today the deity that is allowed access speaks of gnosis. I can feel the being as it seeks words to communicate. There is a sense of being in a nontemporal state in which present, past, and future are one.

As the teaching draws to a close, I feel the familiar sensation of settling back into my body as well as my own thoughts and feelings. The presence of the sacred lingers as the link between the inner and outer realms is experienced.

Just as we ritually open in a certain way, there are specific protocols to close ourselves and the circle. We are charged with not leaving our work in the ritual space, but to integrate and take the experience out into the world. It has been said that in the gnostic tradition, when one climbed the ladder of accension, one was charged with bringing back down that which had been learned and obtained into the community. The Sun sets as the work of the day ends.

• SPIRIT OF CAPRICORN GUIDANCE RITUAL •

Ivo Dominguez, Jr.

The signs are more than useful constructs in astrology or categories for describing temperaments, they are also powerful and complicated spiritual entities. So, what is meant when we say that a sign is a spirit? I often describe the signs of the zodiac as the twelve forms of human wisdom and folly. The signs are twelve styles of human consciousness, which also means that the signs are well-developed group minds and egregores. Think on the myriad of people over thousands of years that have poured energy into the constructs of the signs through intentional visualization and study. Moreover, the lived experience of each person as one of the signs is deposited into the group minds and egregores of their sign. Every Capricorn who has ever lived or is living contributes to the spirit of Capricorn.

The signs have a composite nature that allows them to exist in many forms on multiple planes of reality at once. In addition to the human contribution to their existence, the spirits of the signs are made from inputs from all living beings in our world, whether they are made of dense matter or spiritual substances. These vast and ancient thoughtforms that became group minds and then egregores are also vessels that can be used by divine beings to communicate with humans as well. The spirits of the signs can manifest themselves as small as a sprite or larger than the Earth. The shape and the magnitude of the spirit of Capricorn emerge before you will depend on who you are and how and why you call upon them.

Purpose and Use

This ritual will make it possible to commune with the spirit of Capricorn. The form that the spirit will take will be different each time you perform the ritual. What appears will be determined by what you are looking for and your state of mind and soul. The process for preparing yourself for the ritual will do you good as well. Aligning yourself with the source and core of your energy is a useful practice in and of itself. Exploring your circumstances, motivations, and intentions is a valuable experience whether or not you are performing this ritual.

If you have a practical problem you are trying to solve or an obstacle that must be overcome, the spirit of Capricorn may have useful advice. If you are trying to better understand who you are and what you are striving to accomplish, the spirit of Capricorn can be your mentor. Should you have a need to recharge yourself or flush out stale energy, you can use this ritual to reconnect with a strong clear current of power that is compatible with your core. This energy can be used for magickal empowerment, physical vitality, and healing or redirected for spell work. If you are charging objects or magickal implements with Capricorn energy, this ritual can be used for this purpose as well.

Timing for the Ritual

The prevailing astrological conditions have an impact on how you experience a ritual, the type and amount of power available, and the outcomes of the work. If you decide you want to go deeper in your studies of astrology, you'll find many techniques to pick the best day and time for your ritual. Thankfully, the ritual to meet the spirit of your sign does not require exact timing or perfect astrological conditions. This ritual depends on your inner connection to your Sun sign, so it is not as reliant on the external celestial conditions as some other rituals. Each of us has worlds within ourselves, which include inner landscapes and inner skies. Your birth chart, and the sky that it depicts, shines brightest within you. Although not required, you can improve the effectiveness of this ritual if you use any of the following simple guidelines for favorable times:

+ When the Moon or the Sun is in Capricorn.
+ When Saturn is in Capricorn or making an aspect to a planet in Capricorn.
+ On Saturday, the day of Saturn, and even better at dawn, which is its planetary hour.
+ When Saturn is in Libra where it is exalted.
+ And to a lesser degree of benefit, when Saturn is in Virgo or Taurus.

Materials and Setup

The following is a description of the physical objects that will make it easier to perform this ritual. Don't worry if you don't have all of them; in a pinch, you need no props. However, the physical objects will help anchor the energy and your mental focus.

You will need:

- A printout of your birth chart
- A table to serve as an altar
- A chair if you want to sit during the ritual
- A small dish with three pieces of jet or lodestone to represent the element of earth
- An assortment of items for the altar that correspond to Capricorn or Saturn (some rue, Solomon's seal root or leaf, a piece of lead, and a lily)
- A pad and a pen or chalk and a small blackboard

Before beginning the ritual, you may wish to copy the ritual invocations onto paper or bookmark this chapter and bring the book into the ritual. I find that the process of writing out the invocation, whether handwritten or typed, helps forge a better connection with the words and their meaning. If possible, put the altar table in the center of your space, and if not, then as close to due east as you can manage. Place the dish with the jet or lodestone on the altar and hold your hand over it. Send warming energy from your hand to the stones. Put your birth chart on the altar to one side of the stones and arrange the items that you have selected to anchor the Capricorn and Saturn energy around it. To the other side of the dish, place the pad and pen. Make sure you turn off your phone, close the door, close the curtains, or do whatever else is needed to prevent distractions.

Ritual to Meet the Spirit of Your Sign

You may stand or be seated—whichever is the most comfortable for you. Begin by focusing on your breathing. When you pay attention to the process of breathing, you become more aware of your body, the flow of your life energy, and the balance between conscious and unconscious actions. After you have done so for about a minute, it is time to shift into fourfold breathing. This consists of four phases: inhaling, lungs full, exhaling, and lungs empty. You count to keep time so that each of the four phases is of equal duration. Try a count of four or five in your first efforts. Depending on your lungs and how fast you count, you will need to adjust the number higher or lower. When you hold your breath, hold it with your belly muscles, not your throat. When you hold your breath in fourfold breathing, your throat should feel relaxed. Be gentle and careful with yourself if you have asthma, high blood pressure, are late in pregnancy, or have any other condition that may have an impact upon your breathing and blood pressure. In general, if there are difficulties, they arise during the lungs full or empty phases because of holding them by clenching the throat or compressing the lungs. The empty and full lungs should be held by the position of the diaphragm, and the air passages left open.

After one to three minutes of fourfold breathing, you can return to your normal breathing pattern.

Now close your eyes and move your center of consciousness down into the middle of your chest. Proceed with grounding and centering, dropping and opening, shifting into the alpha state, or whatever practice you use to reach the state of mind that supports ritual work. Then gaze deeply inside yourself and find yourself sitting on a bench in a garden surrounded by standing stones. Look at the beauty of the plants, the stones, and the sky above. Take a breath and smell crisp fresh air. Let the silence of the circle of stones awaken all the places and spaces within you that are of Capricorn. When you feel ready, open your eyes.

Zodiac Casting

If you are seated, stand if you are able and face the east. Slowly read this invocation aloud, putting some energy into your words. As you read it, slowly turn counterclockwise so that you come full circle when you reach the last line. Another option is to hold your hand over your head and trace the counterclockwise circle of the zodiac with your finger.

I call forth the twelve to join me in this rite.
I call forth Aries and the power of courage.
I call forth Taurus and the power of stability.
I call forth Gemini and the power of versatility.
I call forth Cancer and the power of protection.
I call forth Leo and the power of the will.
I call forth Virgo and the power of discernment.
I call forth Libra and the power of harmony.
I call forth Scorpio and the power of renewal.
I call forth Sagittarius and the power of vision.
I call forth Capricorn and the power of
   responsibility.
I call forth Aquarius and the power of innovation.
I call forth Pisces and the power of compassion.
The power of the twelve is here.
Blessed be!

Take a few deep breaths and gaze at the dish with the three stones. Become aware of the changes in the atmosphere around you and the presence of the twelve signs.

Altar Work

Pick up the printout of your birth chart and look at your chart. Touch each of the twelve houses with your finger and push energy into them. You are energizing and awakening your birth chart to act as a focal point of power on the altar. Put your chart back on the altar when it feels ready to you. Then take the pad and pen and write the glyph for Capricorn again and again. The glyphs can be different sizes, they can overlap, you can make any pattern with them you like so long as you pour energy into the ink as you write. Scribing the glyph is an action that helps draw the interest of the spirit of Capricorn. Periodically look at the stones as you continue scribing the glyph. When you feel sensations in your body such as electric tingles, warmth, shivers, or something that you associate with the approach of a spirit, it is time to move on to the next step. If these are new experiences for you, just follow your instincts. Put away the pen and paper and pick up the sheet with the invocation of Capricorn.

Invoking Capricorn

Before beginning to read this invocation, get in touch with your feelings. Think on what you hope to accomplish in this ritual and why it matters to you. Then speak these lines slowly and with conviction.

> *Capricorn, hear me, for I am born of the world's cardinal earth.*
>
> *Capricorn, see me, for the Capricorn Sun shines upon me.*
>
> *Capricorn, know me as a member of your family and your company.*
>
> *Capricorn, know me as your student and your protégé.*
>
> *Capricorn, know me as a conduit for your power.*
>
> *Capricorn, know me as a wielder of your magick.*
>
> *I am of you, and you are of me.*
>
> *I am of you, and you are of me.*
>
> *I am of you, and you are of me.*
>
> *Capricorn is here, within and without.*
>
> *Blessed be!*

Your Requests

Now look inward for several deep breaths, and silently or aloud welcome the spirit of Capricorn. Pick up one of the pieces of jet or lodestone. Close your eyes and ask for any guidance that would be beneficial for you and listen. It may take some time before anything comes through, so be patient. I find it valuable to receive guidance before making a request so that I can refine or modify intentions and outcomes. Consider the meaning of whatever impressions or guidance you received and reaffirm your intentions and desired outcomes for this ritual.

It is more effective to use multiple modes of communication to make your request. Speak silently or aloud the words that describe your need and how it could be solved. Visualize the same message but without the words and project the images on your mind's screen. Then put all your attention on your feelings and your bodily sensations that have been stirred up by contemplating your appeal to the spirit of Capricorn. Once again wait and use all your physical and psychic senses to perceive what is given. At this point in the ritual if there are objects to be charged, touch them or focus your gaze on them.

Offer Gratitude

You may be certain or uncertain about the success of the ritual or the time frame for the outcomes to become clear. Regardless of that, it is a good practice to offer thanks and gratitude to the spirit of Capricorn for being present. Also, thank yourself for doing your part of the work. The state of heart and mind that come with thanks and gratitude make it easier for the work to become manifest. Thanks and gratitude also act as a buffer against the unintended consequences that can be put into motion by rituals.

Release the Ritual

If you are seated, stand if you are able and face the east. Slowly turn clockwise until you come full circle while repeating the following or something similar.

> *Return, return oh turning wheel to your starry home.*
> *Farewell, farewell honorable Capricorn until we*
> *speak again.*

Another option while saying these words is to hold your hand over your head and trace a clockwise circle of the zodiac with your finger. When you are done, snuff out the candle on the altar and say,

> *It is done. It is done. It is done.*

Afterward

I encourage you to write down your thoughts and observations of what you experienced in the ritual. Do this while it is still fresh in mind before the details begin to blur. The information will become more useful over time as you work more with the spirit of Capricorn. It will also let you evaluate the outcomes of your workings and improve your process in future workings. This note-taking or journaling will also help you dial in any changes or refinements to this ritual for future use. Contingent upon the guidance you received or the outcomes you desire, you may want to add reminders to your calendar.

More Options

These are some modifications to this ritual you may wish to try:

+ Put together or purchase Capricorn incense to burn during the ritual. A Capricorn oil to anoint the stones or yourself is another possibility. I'm providing one of my oil recipes as a possibility.

* Set up a richer and deeper altar. In addition to adding more objects that resonate to the energy of Capricorn or Saturn, consecrate each object before the ritual. You may also want to place an altar cloth on the table that suggests Capricorn, Saturn, or the element of earth.

* Creating a sigil to concentrate the essence of what you are working toward would be a good addition to the altar.

* Consider adding chanting, free-form toning, or movement to raise energy for the altar work and/or for invoking Capricorn.

* If you feel inspired, you can write your own invocations for calling the zodiac and/or invoking Capricorn. This is a great way to deepen your understanding of the signs and to personalize your ritual.

Rituals have greater personal meaning and effectiveness when you personalize them and make them your own.

CAPRICORN ANOINTING OIL RECIPE

* * *

Ivo Dominguez, Jr.

This oil is used for charging and consecrating candles, crystals, and other objects you use in your practice. This oil makes it easier for an object to be imbued with Capricorn energy. It also primes and tunes the objects so that your will and power as a Capricorn witch flows more easily into it. Do not apply the oil to your skin unless you have done an allergy test first.

Ingredients:

+ Carrier oil—1 ounce
+ Cypress—6 drops
+ Patchouli—5 drops
+ Bergamot—4 drops
+ Vertiver—4 drops
+ Nutmeg—2 drops

Pour one ounce of a carrier oil into a small bottle or vial. The preferred carrier oils are almond oil or fractionated coconut oil. Other carrier oils can be used. If you use olive oil, the blend will have a shorter shelf life. Ideally use essential oils, but fragrance oils can be used as substitutes. Add the drops of the essential oils into the carrier. Once they are all added, cap the bottle tightly and shake the bottle several times. Hold the bottle in your hands, take a breath, and pour energy into the oil. Visualize silver-gray energy with sparks or repeat the word *Capricorn* or raise energy in your preferred manner. Continue doing so until it feels warm, seems to glow, or you sense that it is charged.

Label the bottle and store the oil in a cool, dark place. Consider keeping a little bit of each previous batch of oil to add to the new batch. This helps build the strength and continuity of the energy and intentions you have placed in the oil. Over time, that link makes your oils more powerful.

BETTER EVERY DAY: THE WAY FORWARD

Maria Wander

"I utilize" is the rallying call of Capricorn, and we really mean it. The process of self-improvement and self-reflection is an integral part of our growth and success. We recognize the positive and negative experiences we encounter, using them as fuel to drive us toward our objectives. Each step we take toward our goals brings a sense of exhilaration and motivates us to keep going. Just as ants diligently carry one grain at a time to build a significant mound, we approach our interests with slow, steady dedication and persistence.

Keep the Faith

When Capricorns are wholehearted in pledging ourselves to mastering our chosen fields, enhancement of our skills through consistent effort is a sacrament. We use our inherent earth power to grow in alignment with our inner awareness, following our calling to a unique purpose. As we listen to that inner voice, it becomes louder and clearer. Social pressures to conform can cause each of us to doubt and quiet this inner guidance. As witches, we have already empowered ourselves to walk our own path. Trust the calling of spirit; it is the part us that seeks to give guidance toward the highest expression of our authenticity and destiny. As challenges arise, embrace them as opportunities for growth, knowing that overcoming obstacles will make us better at who we are and what we do.

The satisfaction of a job well done, or a hobby mastered, brings meaningful purpose and for us, true happiness. While we may push ourselves hard and sometimes work long hours, this is a type of tough self-love. By investing in our own development and well-being, we ensure that we have the capacity to support ourselves and those around us.

Set Goals

Someone asked me how Capricorns get so many things done and still have time for rest, recreation, friends, and family. I shared the Capricorn open secret that the optimal course of action is to set clear personal goals. This is super useful; for example, have a question prior to doing a tarot or oracle card divination. Once you have a direction, read the signs and you'll be on the way. Write them down and place them where you can see them every day. Choose practical goals and intersperse them with fun ones that stoke your interest or relax you. Imagine what your life will be like when you get to the goal you seek, and it is realized. Create as detailed a mental image as you can of this future and describe what you are envisioning. What would some steps toward them feel like if you included them as part of your day-to-day? Write as much of this down as you can and then underline the adjectives. *Healthy*, *nurtured*, *strong*, *skilled*, *proficient*, *able*—you choose. As you go through your days, note when things occur that bring you into feeling these descriptors. Give them your full attention. As those good vibes sink in, let them guide you in creating situations that take you closer to that chosen future. In this way, we can really make our dreams come true since good planning involves starting with the end in mind.

By creating the thoughtform of your destination or goal and energizing it by acting as if it were already a success, you're laying down tracks. Rub your hands together to warm and activate them; focus on the goal you set. Then form an energy ball between your palms and push your thoughts into the energy ball, shaping it into a form that will embody your goal. Maybe you want to achieve something that will take training, either mentally or physically. You could shape the form of a laurel wreath, the round of leafy connected branches that symbolizes triumph. Place this down somewhere safe where it won't be disturbed near where you spend a lot of time, like the windowsill by your desk or a prominent mantelpiece or bedside table. Now that you've envisioned and structured the potential, create your plan with a list: state life goals you want to achieve, break these down into monthly tasks and procedures, and come up with daily skills and learning tasks that will support accomplishment. Share each completion to further empower your thoughtform. If this feels like a long row to hoe, know that it very well may be. Capricorns are built for the long haul and the uphill climb. We like short-term gains as much as the next witch, but not more than we like benefiting in the long run. Cap witches are like those children in the landmark study who were offered a marshmallow and asked to wait fifteen minutes without eating the treat. In doing so, they got to double up on the goods afterward. Not every child was able to do so. Following studies showed the ability to hold off immediate gratification correlated with higher test scores and parental assessment of the child as more capable. Those children had built up a habit of patience and matured into that pattern.

Use your list and the power of your passions to stimulate excitement for each item on your list. Feed that excitement into the goal thoughtform. Organize your list to start with what lights you up most. Sort by considering what requires special timing, such as creating a witch garden in the springtime, or create your own timing boundaries, such as learning new skills through summer reading.

Capricorn Habit Spell

For help with completing a project within a particular time frame, create your plan and its steps, then conduct this helpful spell using planetary timing per the earlier chapter.

Items needed:
+ Two taper candles
+ A pencil

Instructions:

Empower and inscribe two votive candles, one for your actions and one for your goal. Place the action taper to the south and goal taper to the north. Every day/week/month according to your personal timetable, do a step of the work as planned and light and bring the two tapers a step closer together. As the candles burn, envision the manifestation of your goal, snuffing them to be ready to repeat for next time.

If you have planned well and stuck by the plan, by the time the two votives have connected to each other, your actions will have achieved your goal. If any obstacles have impeded you along the way, don't brush them off as annoyances but look deeper to see what they are trying to tell you about improving your process.

Rest and Motion

Settling down into a good routine of regular procedures allows us Capricorns to preserve our desired habit of performance. Keep to a practice of introducing measures of rest throughout activity, like a blacksmith striking against metal on an anvil to craft a tool. Between strikes to the metal, smiths purposefully miss and hammer the anvil. This keeps the rhythm steady to plan a next strike, flip the metal over, or readjust the grip while reducing the force through restful beats, which keeps up momentum. When we create a pause, we make space and room for potentiality. That's why some of our best ideas pop in when our minds are at rest—lying in bed, taking a shower, or driving a familiar route.

Since our favorite pastime is often work, Capricorns find we need to take a knee some days in order to reset. Saturn rules the knees and this movement comes naturally to us. We kneel to propose marriage. We kneel to garden as we dig in the earth. We kneel to protest or in contemplation or sacrifice. The word *sacrifice* comes from *sacer*, which means "sacred or holy," and *facio*, "to make, do, or fashion." When we Saturnians find ourselves knee-deep in it is when we realize our pace has faltered and we are out of rhythm with our entelechy, the internal magic that makes us who we are and drives us toward who we are meant to be. Often knee ache becomes an injury when one is

216

capricious, irresponsible, or has pushed past limits of safety and security. Use this daily practice as part of a reliable restorative routine.

Take a Knee

Do a fourfold breath to calm and concentrate your intentions. Start by breathing in for a count of four, holding for a count of four, breathing out slowly for four seconds, and holding without taking another breath for four seconds. Next, take a walk, do knee lifts, or climb stairs. This will move fluid to your joint and displaces focus away from disequilibrium. Stretch your body and yawn to bring more oxygen into your body and move carbon dioxide out. Repeat the fourfold breath and get back on track toward your goals, one step at a time.

Choice Habits

Capricorns are poised for success and success is about creating needed change and making the right choices. What we choose every day is how our habits are built. Good habits pave the way to success. Choose to be thankful for everything that makes you who you are. Choose when and how to help others with your talents and qualities. Acknowledge gratitude and highlight the good in your life, improvements you have enacted, and your achievements, big and small. Write these in a notebook near where you sit most often and make a habit of testifying to the good in your life using these starter prompts.

Book of Good, Better, Best

- The highlight of my day was …
- The highlight of my week was …
- Today I am most grateful for …
- This week I am most grateful for …
- Today I achieved …
- Today I helped …
- This week I achieved …
- This week I was helped …

I like to write one thought on each page. I flip through and review what I've written at the end of each month. Many times, a notable pattern has emerged from this oracle of self, which helped me clarify and update my life goals.

Full Moon Magic, Capricorn Style

John Beckett

When do you do magic? How often do you do magic? For many of us, our answer comes from the line in *The Charge of the Goddess*: "Whenever you have need of anything." There's nothing like a deep emotional need to motivate us to do the work of spellcasting and to generate the passion required to energize a spell.

But what happens when you don't have a deep emotional need at the moment? Or next week? Or next month? Our ordinary needs are best fulfilled through ordinary action. Large existential needs are often better handled with prayer and meditation. I've found myself going months without lighting a candle, drawing a sigil, or visualizing a result.

And then when I encountered a serious need, my skills were rusty. Oh, I still knew what to do and how to do it. But I was out of practice. The spells felt clumsy, and the results were less than ideal.

Like any other skills, magic and witchcraft require regular practice to reach a level of competency—and to maintain that level. Or to increase it.

And so I decided to put my Capricorn traits to good use: I scheduled regular magical workings.

Deciding when to schedule them was easy. There's the rest of that line from *The Charge of the Goddess*: "And better it be when the moon is full." The full Moon is traditionally the time when magic is at its strongest—if you're going to work magic, that's the best time. A monthly cadence is often enough to keep my skills sharp, and long enough to give most spells enough time to work.

Then I needed magical targets. When I started looking for them, I realized I had plenty of ordinary needs that could be met with ordinary effort, but that could use a magical boost. I realized that while asking my gods for their blessings is a good and holy thing, so is adding my own magic to theirs. My lack of regular magical workings wasn't because I had no needs, but because I had too little imagination.

Some of my early full Moon magic brought immediate results. Some of it didn't. And here I leaned on another Capricorn trait: persistence. If the need is great enough to work magic for it once, then it's great enough to work magic for it two or three or nine times. Sometimes I just worked the same spell again. Other times I created a different spell using a different method: a traditional witchcraft spell instead of sigil magic, or vice versa.

I've been working magic at every full Moon for several years now. The results haven't been perfect—nothing ever is—but they've been good. More importantly, my skills are stronger and more refined. And so now when I encounter a serious need, I have the skills I need to deal with it—and the confidence that I can.

CONCLUSION

Ivo Dominguez, Jr.

I hope you are putting what you discovered in this book to use in your witchcraft. You may have a desire to learn more about how astrology and witchcraft fit together. One of the best ways to do this is to talk about it with other practitioners. Look for online discussions, and if there is a local metaphysical shop, check to see if they have classes or discussion groups. If you don't find what you need, consider creating a study group. Learning more about your own birth chart is also an excellent next step. Some resources for study are listed in the back of this book.

At some point, you may wish to call upon the services of an astrologer to give you a reading that is fine-tuned to your chart. There are services that provide not just charts but full chart readings that are generated by software. These are a decent tool and more economical than a professional astrologer, but they lack the finesse and intuition that only a person can offer. Nonetheless, they can be a good starting point. If you do decide to hire an astrologer to do your chart, shop around to find someone attuned to your spiritual needs. You may decide to learn enough astrology to read your own chart, and that will serve you for many reasons. However, for the same reasons that tarot readers will go to someone else for a reading, the same is true with astrological readers. It is hard to see some things when you are too attached to the outcomes.

If you find your interest in astrology and its effect on a person's relationship to witchcraft has been stimulated by this book, you may wish to read the other books in this series. Additionally, if you have other witches you work with, you'll find that knowing more about how they approach their craft will make your collective efforts more productive. Understanding them better will also help reduce conflicts or misunderstandings. The ending of this book is really the beginning of the adventure.

CAPRICORN CORRESPONDENCES

December 21/22–January 19/21

Symbol: ♑

Solar System: Earth, Saturn

Celebration: Winter Solstice

Season: Winter

Day: Thursday

Runes: Nyd, Peorth

Element: Earth

Colors: Black, Blue (Navy, Royal), Brown, Gray (Dark), Green (Dark), Indigo, Red, Violet, White

Energy: Yang

Chakras: Root, Crown

Number: 6, 9

Tarot: Devil

Trees: Aspen, Birch, Cypress, Elder, Elm, Holly, Magnolia, Mimosa, Pine, Rowan, Spruce, Willow, Yew

Miscellaneous Plants: Cinnamon, Patchouli

Herb and Garden: Carnation, Comfrey, Honeysuckle, Jasmine, Poppy, Rue, Sweet Woodruff, Thyme, Vervain

Miscellaneous Plants: Eyebright, Horehound, Patchouli, Sandalwood, Skullcap

Gemstones and Minerals: Agate, Amethyst, Azurite, Beryl, Bloodstone, Carnelian, Cat's Eye, Fluorite, Garnet, Hematite, Jet, Lapis Lazuli, Malachite, Obsidian, Onyx, Quartz (Clear), Rose Quartz, Ruby, Sapphire (Star), Smoky Quartz, Tiger's Eye, Tourmaline (Black, Green), Turquoise, Zircon (Yellow)

Metals: Lead, Silver

From the Sea: Coral (Black)

Animals: Dog, Elephant, Goat, Lion

Birds: Falcon, Goose (Snow), Heron, Owl

Marine Life: Dolphin

Goddesses: Aphrodite, Freya, Gaia, Hecate, Juno

Angel: Auriel

Gods: Agni, Baal, Dionysus, Ea, Enki, Faunus, Freyr, Loki, Pan, Perun, Saturn, Thor

Issues, Intentions, and Powers: Accomplishment, Ambition, Beginnings, Confidence, Concentration/Focus, Cycles, Darkness, Death, Determination, Discipline, Endings, Grounding, Intuition, Love, Lust, Manifestation, Messages/Omens, Negativity, Obstacles, Order/Organize, Patience, Prosperity, Psychic Ability, Responsibility, Skills, Stability, Success, Willpower

Excerpted with permission from *Llewellyn's Complete Book of Correspondences: A Comprehensive & Cross-Referenced Resource for Pagans & Wiccans* © 2013 by Sandra Kynes.

RESOURCES

Online

Astrodienst: Free birth charts and many resources.

* https://www.astro.com/horoscope

Astrolabe: Free birth chart and software resources.

* https://alabe.com

The Astrology Podcast: A weekly podcast hosted by professional astrologer Chris Brennan.

* https://theastrologypodcast.com

Magazine

The Mountain Astrologer: The world's most recognized astrology magazine. Available in print and digital formats.

* https://mountainastrologer.com

Books

* *Practical Astrology for Witches and Pagans* by Ivo Dominguez, Jr.
* *Parkers' Astrology: The Definitive Guide to Using Astrology in Every Aspect of Your Life* by Julia and Derek Parker

- *The Inner Sky: How to Make Wiser Choices for a More Fulfilling Life* by Steven Forrest
- *Predictive Astrology: Tools to Forecast Your Life and Create Your Brightest Future* by Bernadette Brady
- *Chart Interpretation Handbook: Guidelines for Understanding the Essentials of the Birth Chart* by Stephen Arroyo
- *The Charge of the Goddess* by Doreen Valiente, republished by the Doreen Valiente Foundation, 2014

CONTRIBUTORS

We give thanks and appreciation to all our guest authors who contributed their own special Capricorn energy to this project.

Aeptha

Aeptha is a teacher, ceremonialist, and cosmic mediator. While she works with many inner-level contacts, her primary indwelling contact for her school is through the Solar Mystery Tradition. Aeptha is located in Western North Carolina, and she can be contacted on her web page at www.lighthaven.org.

John Beckett

John Beckett is a Druid, a blogger, and the author of *The Path of Paganism* and *Paganism in Depth*. He's been writing, speaking, teaching, and leading public rituals since 2003. John lives in the Dallas–Fort Worth area where he works as an engineer. Visit John at https://www.patheos.com/blogs/johnbeckett/.

M. Belanger

M. Belanger (he/she/they) is an author, singer, game designer, and television personality known for the *Dictionary of Demons* and the *Psychic Vampire Codex*, as well as appearances on the classic ghost-hunting show *Paranormal State*. Founder of the magickal society House Kheperu, Belanger has been teaching magick, energy work, and psychic development for over thirty years. More information can be found at michellebelanger.com.

Dawn Aurora Hunt

Dawn Aurora Hunt, owner of Cucina Aurora Kitchen Witchery, is the author of *A Kitchen Witch's Guide to Love & Romance* and *Kitchen Witchcraft for Beginners*. Though not born under the sign of Capricorn, she combines knowledge of spiritual goals and magickal ingredients to create recipes for all Sun signs in this series. She is a Scorpio. Find her at www.CucinaAurora.com.

Sharon Knight

Sharon Knight is a musician, artist, and magic worker with a deep love for this beautiful jewel of a planet we live on. She creates from an animistic worldview and loves to sing to the sea and the wind and the trees. She believes magic and the arts are interchangeable modes of communion with the soul of nature. Visit Sharon at https://sharonknight.net/.

Sandra Kynes

Sandra Kynes (Midcoast Maine) is the author of nineteen books, including *Mixing Essential Oils for Magic*, *Magical Symbols and Alphabets*, *Crystal Magic*, *Plant Magic*, and *Sea Magic*. Excerpted content from her book, *Llewellyn's Complete Book of Correspondences*, has been used throughout this series. She is a Scorpio. Find her at http://www.kynes.net.

Jason Mankey

Jason Mankey has been practicing Witchcraft for thirty years and has been writing about the Craft for the last ten. He lives with his wife, Ari, in California's Silicon Valley. Like Doreen, Jason was born on January 4. Visit Jason at https://www.patheos.com/blogs/panmankey/.

Nicholas Pearson

Nicholas Pearson is one of today's leading voices in crystal healing and gemstone magic. He offers a unique blend of science and spirituality alongside a grounded, practical approach to working with crystals. The author of several books, including *Crystal Basics* and *Stones of the Goddess*, he lives in Orlando, Florida. Visit him at https://theluminouspearl.com/.

Notes

Notes

Notes

Notes

Notes

To Write to the Author

If you wish to contact the author or would like more information about this book, please write to the author in care of Llewellyn Worldwide Ltd. and we will forward your request. Both the author and the publisher appreciate hearing from you and learning of your enjoyment of this book and how it has helped you. Llewellyn Worldwide Ltd. cannot guarantee that every letter written to the author can be answered, but all will be forwarded. Please write to:

Ivo Dominguez, Jr.
Maria Wander
℅ Llewellyn Worldwide
2143 Wooddale Drive
Woodbury, MN 55125-2989

Please enclose a self-addressed stamped envelope for reply, or $1.00 to cover costs. If outside the U.S.A., enclose an international postal reply coupon.

Many of Llewellyn's authors have websites with additional information and resources. For more information, please visit our website at:

www.llewellyn.com